ESSAYS ON THE METAPHYSICAL FOUNDATION OF PERSONAL IDENTITY

John A. Reuscher

UNIVERSITY
PRESS OF
AMERICA

LANHAM • NEW YORK • LONDON

Copyright © 1981 by

University Press of America,™ Inc.

4720 Boston Way
Lanham, MD 20706

3 Henrietta Street
London WC2E 8LU England

All rights reserved

Printed in the United States of America

Library of Congress Cataloging in Publication Data

Reuscher, John A.
  Essays on the metaphysical foundation of personal identity.

  1. Ontology—Addresses, essays, lectures. 2. Mind and body—Addresses, essays, lectures. 3. Self (Philosophy)—Addresses, essays, lectures. 4. Interpersonal relations—Addresses, essays, lectures. 5. Identity—Addresses, essays, lectures. I. Title.
BD331.R43   110   80-6067
ISBN 0-8191-1471-5   AACR2
ISBN 0-8191-1472-3 (pbk.)

TABLE OF CONTENTS

                                      Page

PREFACE iii
INTRODUCTION 1

Essay

   1. CLUES 5
   2. SELF-PRESENCE 7
   3. SELF-ACTUALIZATION 11
   4. WORLDS OF THE OTHER 15
   5. WE-CONSCIOUSNESS 27
   6. NAME-CONSCIOUSNESS 35
   7. THE INITIAL QUESTION 41
   8. ALIENATION 65
   9. THE FINAL QUESTION 79
  10. STATES OF MIND AND KNOWING 99

PREFACE

These <u>Essays</u> proceed upon the conviction that wonder about being cannot be satisfied without understanding why this wonder is important. One must why and how mind's wonder about being concerns the being of mind itself. Because of the self-presence of mind's intellectuality it is impossible for it not to pursue the understanding of being as an act vital to its own being or well-being. In short, mind pursues its own being in all that it does, but it does this especially in its effort to understand what it means to be.

Mind, however, does not simply want to be. Mind is conscious that it exists with dignity. That is to say, in virtue of its self-presence, it exists with the authority to be. It is impossible for the existence of mind to be a mere fact. Its interest, therefore, in the question of being possesses the compelling authority of being to be. Mind's interest in what it means to be is a feature of its very act of existing. This interest, however, is important not only because it is vital, but also because it is authoritative, i.e., it is an instance, through mind's self-presence, of being as most authentically itself. Only as self-presence is being fully itself because only so does it fully <u>do</u> its existing as distinguished from merely having it happen. Only as interested in its own being precisely as being at its most authentic can it be serious and authoritative in its attitude toward the question of being.

These <u>Essays</u> proceed also upon the further conviction expressed by Aristotle in the <u>Metaphysics</u> (993a30-993b4):

The investigation of the truth is in one way hard, in another easy. An indication of this is found in the fact that no one is able to attain the truth adequately, while, on the other hand, we do not collectively fail, but everyone says something true about the nature of things, and while individually we contribute little or nothing to the truth, by the union of all a considerable amount is amassed.

This is pre-eminently the case in regard to the truth about mind's interest in both its own being and in being as such. Consequently, these **Essays** reflect the influence of my own meditations upon the texts of Aristotle, Thomas Aquinas, and Kant. Nevertheless, they are not primarily reflections on these writings much less are they an attempt at commentary or synthesis. Although these reflections have been certainly enlightened by these texts, they may not be and certainly do not claim to be at all points congruent with them. Congruence and synthesis were not my purpose. My purpose has been to state for the reader the results of my own reflections on the interpersonal relationship and thereby possibly cast the light a bit beyond where he may stand in his own reflections.

I have selected the genre of the essay because it seems to adapt itself more flexibly to the peculiar structure of this material. That is to say, through the device of a series of Essays one can talk around a subject and thereby produce a gradual progressive clarification of a topic whose natural structure, at least in my opinion, simply cannot be made to yield to the form of a treatise. In any case, I ask the reader's patience with this apparently unsystematic method on the ground that in the course of the exposition it should become clear why this subject resists a more structured literary format.

INTRODUCTION

Since the reflections contained in these _Essays_ claim to be metaphysical, it may be useful to provide the reader in advance with both a specification of what I understand by the word "metaphysical" and a sketch of the metaphysics that does, as a matter of fact, serve as their own particular perspective. On the other hand, since these _Essays_ are not a treatise on metaphysics itself, but rather reflections on the interpersonal relation from a particular metaphysical point of view, I feel it would be out of place and distracting to offer a defense of the contents of this sketch other than to call the reader's attention to their unusual congruence with our intuitions in regard to the matters under consideration.

I take those investigations to be metaphysical which aim at throwing some light on the ultimate conditions required for being precisely as being to make sense. I would also call those investigations metaphysical which attempt to determine the ultimate source of mind's vital interests and the ultimate grounds for their satisfaction. I take these to be complementary ways of approaching the question of the ultimate ground of intelligibility because in such investigations the intelligibility of being is neither clear nor complete until its relation to mind as such has been understood. I accept the view that the mind, precisely because it is intellectual, wants to know upon what its well-being ultimately rests and that as such it is in full possession of the capacity for satisfying this vital curiosity. I also accept the view that being, looked at in the proper perspective, is clear and that its clarity reveals its intelligibility.

The fundamental metaphysical view in these _Essays_ is that of existing as act and perfection.

To be is to do that which we call "being." This is perfection because it is actuality. It is perfection precisely in its serious and interesting sense of authenticity. It is something being what it is supposed to be. And on the most fundamental level, it is being doing what being does, i.e., exist.

Being in this sense of a doing, an acting, has a shape or a form that provides its unity or is its unity. This or that thing does its act in a certain way according to a certain form. In every case, however, the act itself is the same: to exist. That is what is being done or going on. But the way this is done differs from being to being or, at least, from kind of being to kind of being. Now within this variety of forms some are clearly more congenial to this act simply becuase they permit the act greater scope to be itself. The form according to which a bird does its act of existing is obviously more connatural to the act of existing than is the form of a blade of grass because more of what existing is capable of is realized through the former.

Now I take the view in these _Essays_ that the act of existing must, at least in one instance, be structured by a form that is perfectly suited to it in the sense that this form in no way limits or restricts the scope of its perfection. In other words, there must be an instance of the act of existing that is absolutely authentic, i.e., completely itself. There must be an instance of this act in which its form is in such perfect harmony with what it is doing that it is this form. In brief, there must exist a being whose form is simply to be. If this were not so, to exist would not make ultimate sense since it clearly cannot be intelligible in terms of that which hems it in with limitations and it certainly cannot be intelligible through itself as less than itself. Nothing makes sense in terms of its negation.

What I am trying to do through the reflections in these _Essays_ is bring the reader to see that there are very special characteristics that show up in the substantial existence of people who act according to the form of personality, i.e., are personal in their relations with others, that warrant the philosophical suspicion that this form bears some peculiar affinity to the act of existing. It is the interest and objective of these reflections to enquire into this affinity from the metaphysical perspective described above. I try to explicate the connection between mind being this way and the act of existence as such.

The route that is followed in this explication begins with a consideration of being precisely as mind being present to itself. This whole business, however, becomes immediately complicated because two things must be talked about together. We must talk about mind as looking for something and we must talk about mind as being something. These issues are obviously inseparable precisely what mind is decisively determines what it is looking for. Mind is a way of existing that is both a presence to itself and a looking for something in itself through its relation to other subjects. In this regard I try to show that the ultimate unity of mind precisely as mind requires the actuality of an interpersonal relation. In other words, the actuality of personality is the actuality of the ultimate unity mind precisely as mind requires the actuality of an interpersonal relation. In other words, the actuality of personality is the actuality of the ultimate unity of mind.

I accept the view that substantiality is the most authentic status of being and that the form of personality, because of the special unity of the self-presence of its intellectuality, provides the most perfect actualization of the unity of substance. I therefore take the form of personality as that which, given the convertability of unity and being, is the most congenial and connatural to the act of existing. As a consequence, it must be found to be in some transcendent way actualized in that act of existence whose essence is "to be." This would be a self-sufficiently interpersonal reality whose entire actuality is to be the interpersonal relations that constitute its identities.

Finally, the peculiar ontological characteristics that show up in otherwise historically contingent relationships could then be explained on the ground of their similarity to that being whose essence is to exist and whose act of existing is its act of being personal. Finite subjects in their relating produce contingent likenesses of this reality and, consequently, similitudes of its own distinctive existential character show up in these portraits. In other words, through the actualization of the form of personality, the substantial existence of finite contingent subjects enjoys a limited participation by similitude in the mode of existence of the being that is the full actuality of to exist.

The ultimate question, then, to which metaphysics leads is: can a finite subject have a personal relationship with such a being. An attempt to give the gist of my response to this question would require a detail that goes beyond the proper limits of an introduction. It is, nevertheless, well within those limits and indeed essential to the business of this introduction to state that I take the question to be the end of metaphysics in the sense that its answer is that to which the seriousness of mind inevitably moves and beyond which, at least on its own resources, metaphysics cannot go. So, with these thoughts in place, we may now proceed to the first <u>Essay</u>.

ESSAY 1

CLUES

The human being awakes into consciousness to discover itself in a predicament. In the fore of its attention is the unavoidable fact that it is a being of needs. And at the center of this attention is the fact that some of these needs are part of or involved in its very consciousness of itself as a subject. Further, it is clear that these special needs upon the satisfaction of which its whole sense of well-being as subject depends will be met, if at all, by acting in time.

Time, at least the time in which we act, has a "shape." That is to say, the range of possibilities for action changes by the passage of time and is changed by the consequences of action or even the refusal to act. Consequently, the shape of time gives an urgency to the task of understanding the special needs of the subject and what one must do to meet these needs. Mistakes can result in a "time trap," i.e., the situation in which the real available possibilities for the kinds of actions in question have diminished to near zero. It is absolutely important, therefore, to know what these needs are and understand how they can be met.

On the tentative assumption, therefore, that human feelings provide some kind of reliable information about the human subject, we may consult our reactions to the following descriptions.

(1) The consideration of oneself as existing without any friends or in a state of total personal isolation is deeply frightening. No amount of anything else in the whole world could begin to compensate for lonliness. Lonliness is so awful that one would rather not be at all than be in that

state without real hope of change.

(2) The consideration of one's life in any of its central aspects as being out of one's control is frightening. The human subject urgently needs a sense of having his life under control. The loss of control in some way is a loss of one's being as a subject.

(3) The thought of one's life as having no significance or importance causes anger. I want the fact that I have lived to be worth something. I need to make a difference.

(4) The consideration of being used without respect produces fury.

(5) The consideration of being in love is the most attractive thought of which the human mind is capable. One perceives this state as better than anything else in the world. Indeed, its worth is seen to be not only greater than, but even totally other than, any other possible value.

(6) The good person is attractive even if he has lost due to the passage of time or even a calamity virtually all the possibilities for action we normally consider important to life. We perceive the state of being a good person as peaceful and in some sense as absolute. We naturally wish we were that way.

Taken collectively, the feelings portrayed in these scenes would seem to indicate a dependence of one's relation to oneself on a relation to something or someone other than oneself. Without the imposition of a possibly distorting interpretation on these feelings, it may be said that they indicate that the urgency of our needs as subjects imposes itself on certain relations to that which is not ourselves. What follows is an attempt to bring conceptual clarity to this situation.

ESSAY 2

SELF-PRESENCE

If mind looks at itself and attends to the variety of its states, it can become explicitly conscious of the identity of the looking in reference to which it associates all these states as its own. Or, if mind looks at itself and attends to the movement within consciousness, it can again become explicitly conscious of the unity of the looking in reference to which this movement has continuity. However, in both of these exercises, we become aware that in this looking mind is present to itself, is self-conscious. And in fact, it is this very self-presence of mind in the looking that makes its looking at the variety and process in consciousness unifying. Without this self-presence, the looking could not unify because it could not know that it unified. Consciousness can be unified only through a consciousness of unity. Now the word "I" (in use) is a reference to this relation in consciousness of consciousness-as-looking present to itself.

Self-presence is not, however, mind appearing to itself nor is it mind thinking about itself. Self-presence is prior to these activities as the condition of their possibility. In all its actions, no matter what they are about, mind is present to itself. This presence is its being. Mind may indeed explicate this presence as "I," but whether it does so or not, it always remains a presence. That is to say, mind is not merely consciousness _of_ consciousness; it is self-consciousness _in_ consciousness. It is presence in consciousness.

Mind as presence in this sense is both a look (as distinguished from a looking at) and a looking for. By itself it is indeed, precisely as presence, at home, but at home as solitude. It is not merely alone as a matter of fact, it is conscious of itself precisely as being alone. Mind as presence is a look that wants to be seen. As presence to itself it wants to be with another presence. It wants not merely to dwell, but to dwell with. It wants, in other words, to be completely and fully what it is, i.e., presence. Mind, therefore, is conscious of itself as a will to be.

As a will to be, mind is also a will to be reflectively clear to itself so that it can see in what ways it is possible and necessary for it to actualize itself. Mind is, therefore, in virtue of itself as will to be, introspective. In other words, it is essential to the life of the mind that it study itself for the purpose of finding out what it needs to do in order to be fully actual. This is, of course, a special cognitive event because it occurs within self-presence itself. It is an act of knowing about that occurs within the actuality of self-presence and is, indeed, as such, an explication of self-presence. More precisely, it occurs within the explication of self-presence in the I-act. It is an act of knowing about that is illuminated by the knower's will to be self-presence. The vital urgency of the will to be makes mind introspectively clear to itself in the immediacy of its self-presence. Its act of being, for the moment, is its act of willing to see itself--this is how it is present to itself--and this actuality is its clarity. Since this kind of cognitive act is different from all other kinds of both because of the peculiar existential relationship between knower and known and also because of the peculiar ontological structure of that which is to be known, it seems useful to say something here about this mode of understanding.

We differentiate between diagramatic and nondiagramatic understanding. The former employs or can employ the logical properties of the constitutive relations of space and time to interpret both the structures of states of affairs and the distinction of our awareness of them from their existence and composition. Nondiagramatic understanding, on the other hand, cannot use spatio-temporal relations as interpretive instruments because it is concerned about states of affairs in which there is a structure the logical property (or properties) of whose relations is not compatible with the logical properties of the former. Such relations can, indeed, be represented, but not by diagrams or pictures.

The understanding of mind is nondiagramatic. Meanings can be pictured, but not mind. Thought is a mode of mind's self-presence. In thought, mind is aware of itself in its concern for that which is other than thought. It is also aware of itself in its concern for the memory of thoughts. And, finally, it is aware of itself in its concern for itself as relating to thinking as activity. Thinking about mind is, therefore, the explication of the self-presence involved in all thought. It is not a separate act, but rather a shift of attention within an act. In other words, that which is being thought about is actualized in and thereby captured in the act of thinking. It is a looking at something in the act by that which thinks. The self-presence which produces the thought, and which is what the thought is about, is in the thought as a mode of its actuality.

This situation cannot be pictured; it can only be pointed to. There is no image for this reality. Just as there are no boxes that can be inside themselves, nor items that can be beside themselves, nor parts coextensive with the whole, and as there are no moments that follow themselves or are before themselves, so there are no spaces and no times that can represent self-presence and thinking about self-presence. There are, therefore, no separate elements in self-presence. Just as there is no inside or outside, so there are no parts. In no sense and in no way can this relation be thought through the model of "being next to."

Self-presence is nondiagramatic and lies, therefore, outside the domain of diagramatic understanding. It is a unique relational state to which attention can be called but for which there is no adequate concept. Only self-presence can represent self-presence, and it can do this explicitly only through the Ego that is involved in every thought. This mode of thought uses an instance rather than a concept as the focus of its attention. It provides, therefore, only ostensive statements. Self-consciousness in thinking about itself can only exhibit itself in this thinking as an instance for the purpose of clarification through explication.

We move now to the introspective clarification the self-presence of mind.

ESSAY 3

SELF-ACTUALIZATION

The nondiagramatic relation of mind's self-presence is dynamic, and dynamic precisely as a nondiagramatic self-actualization. This relation according to the specific modes of its existence is actualized and sustained in its actuality through the subject's activity of relating as self-presence to the other than itself. In other words, the subject as self-presence is a relation that is itself the originating term of the activity of relating to the other than itself, and the actuality of its existence depends upon the success of this relating. The relation of self-presence is an act that is sustained <u>in</u> the act of relating to the other. The actuality <u>of</u> the relation of self-presence is the act of being present to self. This act occurs in the act of relating to the other than the self. The subject must relate to the other in order to be itself, i.e., self-presence. I am, in brief, a self-present relator.

On the other hand, it is evident that from another perspective all relating to the other depends on the actuality of self-presence. It is, after all, precisely as self-present that I relate to the other. The whole situation of the subject is, therefore, nondiagramatic. The actuality of the relation of self-presence and the actuality of its relation to the other than itself are reciprocally dependent.

Now this reciprocal dependence sets the formula for the self-actualization of the subject. Whatever the subject is to be or become, it can do so only within the economy of its relating to the other than itself. All of its vital interests are, therefore, in a fundamental way attached to this formula and all that follows both in this and the subsequent essays serves merely for the clarification of why this is so and the explication of the conditions of its implementation.

The fundamental modes of the existence of the self-presence of mind are knowing and willing. These are obviously not the only modes of mind as act, but they do appear to be in a special way distinctive of the subject in its relation to itself. Mind is self-present as self-knowing and as self-determining possession. In other words mind stands in its own presence as knowing itself and possessing itself. These are the ways it is actually a self-relating. These modes are also nondiagramatic.

Now the perfection of knowledge depends, at least in part, on the actuality and clarity of the existence of that which is known. Likewise, the perfection of possession depends, again at least in part, on the existential stability of that which is possessed. And this is true whether the known and possessed is the self or the other than self. Actuality is the determining factor. We may say, therefore, that the perfection of the mind's self-presence precisely because of these two primary modes of this presence depends directly upon the actuality of the existence of this relation. Again, this is a nondiagramatic situation. The perfection of the presence of the subject in itself is both dependent upon and is the actuality of the subject.

As we, however, have already seen, the actuality of self-presence depends upon the actuality of the self relating to the other. We may conclude, therefore, that the actuality required for the perfection of self-presence according to its primary modes of knowing and possession depends upon the actuality of the subject's relation to the other.

The mind is, however, present to itself as a will to be. This will to be is the self-present power of consciousness to be to the fullest according to the modes of its existence. It is, in other words, the will to be self-presence perfectly as self-knowing and self-determination. This is the absolute seriousness of being. In the light of what has been said above, however, we can see why this will is equivalently the will to relate to the other. The actuality that determines the perfection of self-knowledge and self-possession is a function of the actuality of the subject's relating to the other. I must relate in order to be self-present. This is the source of the seriousness of the will to relate to the other. It is also, as we shall try to show in Essay 9, a manifestation of the imperative of being to be as legitimating the demand to be allowed access to the other by the other.

We now ask in a general way and for the purpose of completing this initial description of the dynamics of self-presence what sort of relationship to the other offers the subject the prospect of its greatest actualization. Provisionally, at least, this would seem to be the relation of perfect mutual identification. It would seem, after all, that the relation in which the unity between the relata is such that there is only that much difference as may be required for there to be a relation at all, i.e., a purely relational altereity, which would indeed be the most perfect precisely because it calls for the greatest possible unity between real altereities. The relation of perfect similitude of real altereity in existential oneness would seem to be the ultimate in the order of relationships. This would, of course, be perfect identification. This would be a relation so perfect that the whole actuality of the relata would consist in a single simple collaborative act of being mutually to the other, of being "inter." In this situation the actuality of the relata as other would consist precisely in their mutual attitude toward one another in an existentially simple act of self-presence. They would be correlative relations of "being-to-the-other" as subsisting in a single act of existence. And it might very well be the case that since the unity is absolutely perfect, the necessity of the existence of this act would also be absolute. This might be the absolute actualization of mind's self-presence in regard to unity and necessity. It would be the ideal of interpersonality.

We must, of course, assert that it does appear to be the case that the existential limitation of the human being is such that it is not self-sufficiently intersubjective. It does not discover within the act of its consciousness a real other than itself. In itself, although present to itself, the human mind is alone. In itself, it looks for but is not seen by another. Within itself, no real relation of mutual identification would seem to be possible. By itself, the human mind does not possess the self-sufficient resource for its maximal actualization in a relation of mutual identification. It would seem therefore that the human mind is incapable of the kind of perfect relation and absolute actualization described above.

As I intend to show however in Essays 7 and 9, it does not follow from this limitation that the possibility and, indeed, actuality of the absolutely perfect relationship of mutual identification is a matter of indifference to the human being or is, perhaps at most, a speculative curiosity. And it most certainly does not follow that there cannot be a relation of identification within the existential limits of the human situation that is capable of fully meeting the mind's interest in the greatest actualization of which it is capable. In fact this is precisely what it is I want to show in these Essays. What does follow is that because of the ontological seriousness and urgency of the will to be, the human mind is a restless anxious problem to itself until it has found this relationship.

We can now turn our attention to the fundamental kinds of worlds of relating.

ESSAY 4

WORLDS OF THE OTHER

The subject finds itself in two worlds for relating. One is the world of items for use, i.e., things. The other is the world of self-presences, i.e., subjects. In both cases, the mode of relating will be determined by both the modes of the existence of the relating subject and the modes of the existence of the populations of these two worlds for relating. The complete being of the relating subject itself inhabits both worlds although, obviously, in different respects. This observation is important because, as I will eventually try to show, the unity of the full life of the being of this subject depends upon its successful integration of these two worlds in its relating activity.

A. <u>The World of Things</u>

I am conscious of an effort on the part of mind as cognitive to understand things and events, and I am conscious of this effort as being urgent. From mere frustrated curiosity to suicidal anxiety, the failure of this effort is never a matter of indifference. That this is so is due to the fact that the mind is conscious of itself as being in the presence of states of affairs that are structured or held together by relations with the mode of necessity, and that somehow its apprehension of this necessity is absolutely vital to its own unity. This situation may be explicated in the following way.

The necessity of the structuring relations appears with varying degrees of clarity. These variations in clarity are due to the fact that in these matters the mind must contextualize in order to see, and the most appropriate context or frame may be discovered only gradually (at least in some cases). This viewing of things in context permits their translation into corresponding mental equivalents called meanings and reasons. The subject has an absolute interest in the success of this activity because as a consciousness of its consciousness of states of affairs, its unity (which is a fundamental mode of its existence) is a function of the unity of its consciousness of the other. Indeed, the unity of the activity of understanding and the unity of the subject that understands are nondiagramatic mutual conditions of one another.

These unities of states of affairs are, then, patterns of relations as contextually necessary. And through understanding the relating subject itself becomes contextually necessary in the sence that it belongs to this world to which it relates as making sense. I make sense to me because my world makes sense to me. But for me to be meaningful in this way is a fundamental mode of my being as subject. Therefore, I will to understand.

The subject is furthermore conscious of an effort on the part of mind as power or will to control states of affairs, i.e., to make sure they make sense according to a context that includes the subject. The sensed urgency of this concern I take to be another aspect of the same vital equation described above, but in this instance the subject is self-possessor rather than self-knower. In this case, the result is unity through power rather than unity through understanding. Indeed, loss of power over one's state of affairs is frightening precisely because it is a direct threat to this fundamental mode of the very existence of the subject as self-presence, and at least an indirect threat to the subject's aspect as a thing.

To the extent that this relating activity is successful the subject derives a sense of being an object that makes sense in a world that works. It gains what might be called operational clarity and stability. It can count on its health, its financial picture, its safety, etc. This clarity and stability provide a limited although essentially important actualization of the subject's relation to self-presence, and, consequently, a limited possibility for its actualization as self-knower and self-possessor.

In both of these kinds of relating activities, there is a radical inadequacy in the result relative to the ultimate interest of the subject. In both cases, the contexts that generate the unities are "thing" contexts. The states of affairs are situated in a "thing-frame." That is to say, they are viewed not only as other than the self-consciousness of the subject, but also as not self-conscious at all.

Within this frame of reference, although states of affairs can be seen to be meaningful, the meaningfulness of reality so viewed does not reveal why anything exists at all and, therefore, does not reveal why anything that does exist should not exist. In other words, this is a frame of reference within which ways of existing can be understood, but not the fact of existence itself. Within this frame, therefore, it is possible for the subject to give itself the unity of that kind of necessity which is a function of the relations among beings and modes of being, but always being merely as thing. It gives itself the unity and necessity of being the subject of a reality as thing in a world of things.

This relational activity, however, cannot provide the subject with that which the world of things does not possess, or at least does not show itself as possessing, namely, existential necessity. The world of things shows itself to be something that works and can be counted upon to do so for the foreseeably interesting future. It does not, however, show itself as existing necessarily. No inspection of things shows that they have to be. They are facts, and as such they must ultimately disappoint the subject. The subject is a will to be perfectly according to the modes of its existence. But to be perfectly self-knower, the knowing requires for its perfection the existential significance of the self to be known. This means that it wants its existence to have some degree of necessity that can lift it beyond the ultimate triviality of a mere fact. Self-inspection by the subject, however, discovers no such necessity, at least as a <u>datum</u>. If it is to be there at all, it must somehow be acquired. Hence the subject's unavoidable ultimate disappointment in its knowledge of things. They simply cannot provide it with precisely that which it needs and wants most for its own fullest actualization, i.e., existential necessity.

The same can be said for the subject's power over things. They cannot provide the existential necessity it needs for the fullest actualization of the relation of self-presence as possession. They consequently leave its grip on itself unsatisfactorily fragile. Possessing can only be as actual or perfect as the existential stability of that which is possessed. The self as an unnecessary event can be only imperfectly possessed. In self-possession, the consciousness of the possessing which is indeed the possessing is a direct function of the consciousness of the existence possessed which is also the existence itself. The ultimate satisfaction, therefore, of the subject's most urgent will to be must be achieved, if at all, in the world of other subjects.

B. The World of Subjects

Besides being aware of states of affairs as thing-situations, the subject is aware that it is also confronted by other self-present minds. In this confrontational situation there is a mutual look that reveals and recognizes the presence and similitude of self-presences to one another. We are immediately aware that this state of mind is radically different from that of "thinking about." One can, of course, retreat from the confrontation into a posture of thinking about, but one cannot stay in the confrontation without doing something different from the understanding and use of a thing.

The mode of the subject's relating in the world of subjects will be determined, of course, by the peculiarities of the mode of the existence of self-presence. First of all, unlike things, the domain of self-presence is one of radical privacy. How I am in my self-presence, i.e., my attitudes, can never be understood in the sense of figured out with necessity and certainty. Self-presence as such is privacy. I am not, by the way, talking here about the freedom of self-presence. This would concern the nonpredictability of attitudes. I am talking about the character of my presence to my mind states regardless of the nature of their origin. This is the ultimate intimacy of mind's relation to itself in which it is present to all its states and thereby stands behind them both looking out through them and also looking at them. It is the character of this latter attitude that can never be computed from the outside precisely because it is a radical nondiagramatic "inside." It is totally beyond the reach of "outside" as such. This attitude is a secret precisely because self-presence is secret.

Cognitive relating between self-presences precisely as such can never, therefore, be merely or even primarily informational. There must be a revelation. There must be a communication that is a telling of the secret. But the curious thing about the secret is that it contains the communicator. This kind of communication is always a mystery. Something that can never be figured out is made crystal clear precisely because the act by which it is to itself, i.e., the act by which it is actual, is now the act of saying, i.e., the act by which it is to the other. That is, of course, exactly why one becomes so vulnerable in this kind of communication. One literally makes oneself the content of the message. The act of communicating is the substance of what is said and, as such, contains the self-presence of the sayer. It is the actuality of the speaker. The clarity of the actuality of this self-presence is itself the clarity of and in the communication because the act of communicating is in this instance the actuality of the subject's self-presence.

Now it must be obvious that such a revelation asks for and rightfully expects an equally special sort of response. It asks for and expects a response in which the act of accepting the revelation is, like the revelation itself, an act identical with the actuality of the responder's self-presence. It looks, in other words, for an act of faith. It looks for an act which is itself an equivalent revelation that in itself calls for faith; it looks for belief that is itself a revelation calling for belief. The original revelation expresses, therefore, the will to believe the believer.

The reader's attention is here called to a point of the greatest importance which will be developed in Essay 5. The complex act of communicating as carrying both the revelation of self-presence and the will to believe depends for its perfection and continuance on mutuality. Without a corresponding communication on the part of the other this act cannot be sustained and brought to perfection because there would be no one for it to speak to and nothing for it to believe. In short, there would be no communication at all. But this act because of its message is in a unique manner directly supportive of the actuality of self-presence and is, indeed, a manifestation of that actuality. The mutuality produces, therefore, a peculiar nondiagramatic unity between the participating subjects. There is now a mutual dependence of the actualities of the self-presences upon one another. The actualities of the self-presences are, in fact, functions of one another. We have here, therefore, an inchoative similitude of the relation of identification and, thereby, the beginning of the maximal actualization of the subjects. That is why in this situation one has the sense of being most alive. This is also why the will to be translates itself into the will to be believed and to believe.

As might be obvious from what has been said so far (and as we shall try to clarify further in

Essay 10) we believe because we want to be. The ground of this belief is, therefore, ontological. There are, however, two other ways of viewing this matter that highlight and bring to the fore its more specifically metaphysical features. The first concerns the attractiveness of similitude. I see that the other as self-presence is the perfect likeness of myself. I see further that our consciousness of this basic similitude and the attitudes involved in these consciousnesses are alike. This double similitude is the ontological source of the mutual attraction that moves to maximal existential unity. That is to say, it moves toward the maximization of likeness in every aspect of vital importance. It moves to identification. Similitude moves, however, to a unity that overcomes difference as separateness, not difference as otherness. I therefore believe in order to be one with my perfect likeness. As we will see again in Essay 9, there is within being the movement in all of its instances to be itself, and the attractiveness of similitudes among the self-conscious existentially limited instances of itself is a manifestation of this movement. This is the striving of being in self-conscious being to be itself within limits.

The second way of viewing this matter concerns the awesome dignity of the self-conscious subject. In Essay 9 I offer a metaphysical clarification of the ontological source of this distinctive feature of self-consciousness. Here I merely wish to comment on the role of this feature in regard to belief. Intelligence sees in self-presence a worth for which it cannot design an adequate conceptual or interpretive context in relation to which this worth would be generated precisely because it is seen not to be relative at all. It depends on no purpose and has nothing whatsoever to do with the peculiar qualities and circumstances of the individual in which it is found. Indeed, not even the moral goodness (or evil) of the subject has any bearing on it. Intelligence also sees that it cannot comprehend this worth. There is something about being this way that strikes awe and commands absolute respect. Intelligence "senses" it is in the presence of that which somehow intelligence itself is all about and the depth of whose importance it can never fully appreciate and never exhaustively understand.

Now this dignity attaches to the communicative act by which self-presence tries to maximize its actuality, and the consequent corresponding respect for this act is an intrinsic self-sufficient motive for belief. In fact, the dignity of this kind of communication contains an imperative. It <u>ought</u> to be believed. The refusal to believe is a radical evil that somehow strikes at the very worth of being as such. It is the negation of being in its most fundamental act. This is, indeed, ontological evil. It strikes at that very act by which being is or becomes most authentically itself.

Again, because a fundamental mode of the existence of the subject is self-possession, one cannot relate volitionally in the world of subjects by simply taking possession for use. The whole domain of the subject in all its aspects belongs, at least originally, to the self-presence of that subject. The life of the subject is his to do with as he pleases so long, of course, as he does not interfere with the like competence of someone else. The only volitional relation, therefore, that is possible between self-presences is, again, a mutual communication, but in this instance a mutual communication of control over their lives. The degree of control communicated will depend, of course, on the kind of relationship the parties wish to establish. In the case of a relationship of identification, however, the control is virtually total.

As in the case of revelation, the real content of the communication is the subject. The act of giving directly sustains the actuality of the self-presence of the giving subject and thereby contains that subject. And since in this case the mode of relating is control, it is appropriate to call this communication "gift." The actuality of the subject's self-presence as self-possessor is now sustained by the act of possessing a self indeed, but a self that is other, while its own self is indeed possessed, but by the other. In this situation, the actualities of the self-presences are being sustained by the interlocking activity of mutual gift giving. It is for this reason that the gift giving must be mutual, otherwise one party, although possessed as a self, would not be a self-possessor. And because the self-presences are perfect likenesses of each other, this relation moves to identification and the maximal actualization of the subjects.

This kind of relating, however, from the nature of what is communicated calls for a special ontologically crucial attitude on the part of the parties to the relation. If a gift is really a gift, it must be really given, i.e., turned over to the other. It must really become the other's. It must belong to him. It cannot, therefore, simply be taken back. This mode of communicating, therefore, calls for and rightly expects fidelity. This is the firm will to honor the gift. It is, in other words, the perfection of the communication giving it an absolute character that altogether removes it from the world of things and use. In fact, fidelity, as an absolute commitment is, in conjunction with faith, the ontological completion of the relation of identification and, as we shall see shortly, provides the existence of the subject with an authenticity that transcends the bare existential factivity of things. This is being as authentically itself, as most real, i.e., as necessary. But for the moment I want simply to concentrate on fidelity as essential to this mode of relating and on the fact that to be at all, it must be absolute. No relation of identification is possible without it nor is the authentication of the existence of the subject beyond mere factivity. In short, the entire possibility of the fulfillment of the will to be depends directly upon commitment and fidelity. In Essay 8, we examine what this means for freedom.

The motives for fidelity are precisely the same as those for faith, i.e., the will to be, the attractiveness of similitude, and respect for the dignity of self-presence. However, since fidelity stands in a more immediate and direct confrontation with freedom than faith, or at least so it seems, the evenness of the burden on these motives in the former case becomes upset. In the day to day long haul of a serious relationship of identification, it is the motive of respect that eventually must carry the major part of the burden in the endless, tiring, and tiresome struggle with the mind's fascination with its freedom. In the most literal sense I can think of, it can be said that the entire life of the mind, the fulfillment of its deepest and most urgent aspirations, its grip on reality, indeed its very sanity, all depend upon this one absolutely fundamental attitude of respect. This attitude is that basic self-effected realism of mind that protects it from becoming fantastic, ridiculous, and ugly. As I try to show in Essay 8, the absence of this attitude must lead to the ultimate absurdity of self-adoration and then to madness, if by madness is meant total loss of contact with reality.

Fidelity, therefore, as grounded in at least one of its fundamental motives, is absolute. It must be so because the worth of self-presence is seen to be absolute, and to be unfaithful is to treat the other as having only that worth which would be determined by its relation to some purpose or objective. It would be disrespect and, therefore, evil.

In the light of these remarks about faith and fidelity it may now be possible to make some sense out of the very peculiar attractiveness of the relationship of identification for the human mind. This relationship is seen to possess a character of absoluteness. It presents itself as absolutely beautiful, absolutely good, and of absolute value. That is to say, it possesses these qualities simply in itself and in virtue of itself without any reference to anything else. This makes such a situation, of course, intrinsically attractive to mind both because by being party to such a relation it makes itself in its existential particularity beautiful, good, and of absolute worth, and because intellectual mind is interest in the absolute and here this interest is given at least provisional satisfaction.

      The human mind, however, is also drawn to this kind of relationship because of something that is, in a sense, deeper or more fundamental than its beauty, goodness, and worth, something indeed of which these are modes, i.e., existence itself. The mind "senses" an absolute character to the very existence of such a relationship. It ought to be. And this "ought" stands in relation to no condition whatsoever. The relationship quite simply ought to be. I do not here use the word "ought" primarily in a moral sense but rather with an ontological or existential emphasis. For the moment, it will be sufficient to say that I mean that there is a peculiar relation or orientation of the form of the relationship of identification to existence such that it can be said to have a title to exist. In other words there is some sort of connection between the realism of this form in relation to actuality as such, i.e., existence, that it should exist. It somehow contains or participates in the necessity by which there must be something rather than nothing. This is the fundamental necessity of being itself. Or, to put it another way, there is something about actuality as such, that wherever possible and to the extent possible, it should be this way. In some sense, this must be, or comes very close to being, the most perfect way for actuality as such, the closest possible match between form and existence.

      In Essay 9, I return to these considerations for a further clarification through the metaphysical analysis of being. Here, however, it will be sufficient to point out that the mind does feel drawn to this way of being as satisfying its most urgent interest in being. The relationship of identification is attractive because in some way it contains an absolute existential necessity. It is, therefore, absolutely interesting. We can provisonally say that the form of the relationship of identification is the form of actuality as such and that, as a consequence, it carries in itself the necessity of actuality as such. Other forms are limited likenesses or participations in this form and can, therefore, communicate operational necessity or intelligibility to the acts which they structure. They cannot communicate necessity or intelligibility to the existence of the agent. The form of the relationship of identification, on the other hand, precisely because of its relation to actuality as such, gives the very existence of the agent a participated existential necessity. It makes the existence itself absolutely significant and, indeed, to do so is its hallmark or signature.

This significance manifests itself as moral goodness. People who are this way, or at least are of a will to be this way, are properly what we mean by good people. We can now see that moral goodness is really an ontological character that, unlike other kinds of goodness, attaches directly to the existence of the agent in virtue of the form of identification or being personal. We do not, for instance, say that the brilliant scientist is, in virtue of his scientific excellence, a good person. This we reserve exclusively for the human being of real faith and fidelity. And this is why the life of the good man inspite of the loss of perhaps every advantage humans normally covet, remains for the sane mind splendidly attractive. The existence revealed in such a life is absolutely real, fully actual, and, in some serious sense, necessary. It is in the state of moral goodness, and only in this state, that the mind can find the full satisfaction of its will to be. It is only in that state that it possesses the form of actuality as such and thereby achieves full reality, clarity, and stability. This is the mind's fullest actualization according to its modes of being self-knower and self-possessor. It is in this situation that it can say to itself: I am.

ESSAY 5

WE-CONSCIOUSNESS

We have seen that identification is a situation in which the relation of self-presence in several subjects is actualized by other-oriented relating activities that depend on one another for their mutual possibilities. These activities occur and, indeed, only can occur in the situation of the non-diagramatic relation of self-presences conscious of each other, conscious of that consciousness, and conscious of the whole situation. At the end of this essay I offer two symbolic representations designed to give the reader a sense of the complexity of just a fragment of this situation. The situation of several self-presences so present to each other that the "present to each other" is up front in the attention of each is what I want to talk about in this essay. Properly speaking, this situation cannot be thought in the sense of conceptualized. It can, however, be pointed to and thought about, and that limit must determine my method.

"We" is the unifying form of the complex activities of identification. It is the form of the unity of the identification and the form of the consciousness of that unity. As a formal consciousness it is the unity of the activities by which the involved parties maintain the actualities of their respective self-presences. It is, therefore, both the form of the inter-dependent unity of these actualities and the form of the consciousness of that unity. "We" expresses the actuality of a plurality in the order of self-presence in the actuality of a unity in the same order or mode of being, i.e., a self-presence. So it expresses the strong plurality of identities in the unity of a self-presence; it is, indeed, the plurality of subjects in the self-conscious unity of a subject. It is the plurality of the actuality of subjects in the unity of the actuality of the act of a subject.

Unity <u>in</u> this mode of being is possible only <u>through</u> <u>th</u>is mode of being. That is to say, self-consciousness of the unity of subject is the only possible mode of unity of subjects in this order of being. The unity must be of the same ontological mode as that of what is being unified. Self-presences can be unified only in the self-conscious actuality of a common self-presence that is accomplished through participation in an act of being self-present. We are present to us.

To put this matter another way, just as consciousness <u>of</u> the form "I" is indeed unified <u>by</u> that form such <u>th</u>at the act of being conscious is both executed by the "I" and also constitutes the actuality of the "I," so the consciousness <u>of</u> the form "We" is unified <u>by</u> that form in such wise that the interdependent subject sustaining activities of being to the other are both executed by the "We" and also constitute its actuality. In this order of being, the actuality of the formal unity of the consciousnesses of the subjects is the actuality of the unity of the new self-present subject speaking "We." The self-presence <u>is</u> the self-consciousness of the unity accomplished both in and through identification.

We-consciousness, as the explication in identification of its formal unity, stands in an order of being in which its distinctive form has a peculiar relation to existence. This form clearly affects the existence of self-presence and this effect manifests itself directly into the consciousness of self-presence. In other words, the unity of this form somehow provides "scope" for existence to be maximally itself. The existence of a self-presence by itself is thin; it reveals itself as unnecessary and insignificant. It is trivial. The same existence in this form becomes somehow authentically being. It has an integrity, a significance, an importance all of which appear as absolute. This form clearly gives an otherwise contingent existential fact the status of absoluteness. It approaches the fullest self-contained status of being at its best.

It is existence in this form that alone is not simply good without qualification; in virtue of this form it is holy. This is existence that ought to be because it is holy. No other form does this to existence. Nor does any other form give the self-present subject of this existence the sense of absolute peace, freedom, stability, and the sense, in spite of every adversity, of being fully alive. The assertion "We are" in some way involves or points to "and this is <u>to be</u>." In other words, the actuality of "We" seems to present itself to consciousness as having something to do with why there is anything at all or, at least, with what <u>to be</u> is ultimately all about.

The ultimate actualization of the existence of self-presence through the form of identification may, therefore, be called "indwelling." That is to say, this form so unifies the self-presences that they <u>dwell</u> with one another in the existence of We-consciousness. This is a movement toward the strongest authenticity of identity in the strongest unity of existence. The existential strength of one's relation to oneself is a direct function of the existential strength of one's relation to the other in identification. And here is the anomaly. The actuality of one's distinctiveness as self-presence depends upon relating activities whose form moves to the greatest possible existential unity of the subjects. It is in the indwelling of perfect identification that my individuality achieves its greatest actuality and authenticity. It will be the purpose of the next essay to bring this matter to further clarity. For the moment, however, I wish merely to indicate that there seems to be something about being that points to "being with" or "indwelling" as the perfection of being itself. That is to say, it would seem, at least provisionally, that the interdependent acts of relating in identification in which there occurs a reciprocal strengthening of identities and unity of existence has something to do with being as absolute. It would seem that being, at its best and most real, _is_ indwelling.

Finally, it would seem that the strength of the actuality of the existence and unity of We, namely the strength of its identity precisely as We, requires its own "other" with whom it can identify. We, precisely as We, as a unified self-presence, does not want to be alone. As subject, it wants to be with, to be present to another presence. As subject, it needs another to whom it can speak and by whom it can be recognized. We as subject needs the other to whom it can speak itself in mutual acceptance and give itself in mutual commitment. Its distinctive unity is brought to completed actualization in its act of interrelating with another. To put this another way, the actuality of its self-presence precisely as We is completed in its act as subject communicating with another. Indeed, its clarity as self-knower and stability as self-possessor is completed in the interdependent activities of identification with another self-presence. The actuality of this identification is required for the completion of its own reality.

This situation is itself, of course, another We. It is not, however, _just_ another We. It is the completion of the full requirement for the perfect actuality of the self-consciousness of identification. The completion of the unity of the interrelating activities of mutual identification requires that the unity itself act. That is to say, the perfection of the unity achieved through the self-presence expressed in and by We, i.e., the self-presence needed as the form through which self-presence can be completely actualized requires that this unity actualized through such a form itself actively relate in identification with another self-presence. In other words, the complete perfection of the being of this We subject demands that, precisely as We, it must act to another. To be perfectly itself, it must act itself.

The identification accomplished through this act is, as I said, not just another We. This is the full realization or completion of the scope of the actuality of We. To say this another way, the form of the completed situation of identification maximizes the unity and existence of self-presence to its ultimate intrinsic potential. Beyond this is mere repetition, not improvement. We can say, therefore, that it belongs to the complete actualization of the reality of self-presence that there be a We situation in which one identity as relation is completed in its actuality by standing in an identification relation to an originative relation. Or, the complete perfection of identification requires that just as the self-relations of individuals must interrelate, so this interrelation must itself, in order to be fully itself, interrelate. The perfection of existence on the order of self-presence requires, therefore, a structured indwelling in which the complete reality is the actuality of the interdependence of the originative We relation and its relation to its other.

All of this would seem to point to one more thing about being itself, namely, that beyond the completed perfection of identification, there is nothing further for it to do. This is not a limit of being but rather and on the contrary its complete fulfillment of itself. In other words, if instances of this situation are as a matter of fact existentially limited, they are so not by anything having to do with its form. This form clearly has some peculiar connection with existence such that one can say that in the fullest sense of to be or to exist is to be this way. Being and being this way seem ultimately to be the same. Again, as I have said before, this is in some very real sense to be absolutely. That is why the human mind, whose primary interest is being, is absolutely attracted to this mode of existence.

I wish now to conclude this essay by briefly calling the reader's attention to several distinctions of importance. There are three levels, so to speak, of unity that can exist between or among self-presences. The first is found in the situation of mutual awareness in which, however, there is no communication. Chart A at the end of this essay describes the development of unity at this level and Chart B gives a partial description of its complexity. The attitudes in this situation, if any, may indeed be perfectly benign, but since they are not communicated I would not call this level of unity personal. At best, it is merely psychological.

      The second level does involve communication, but only in regard to the world of things. In this situation, the collectivity of shared practical interests results in the We of useful concern. This does not touch, however, what might be called the substantive actuality of self-presence and consequently cannot generate a real unitary self-present We. It only results and can only result in a conventional subject or We, and as such participates in all the limitations of the world of things. Again, although this unity may be quite benign, it is not what I would call personal.

      Finally, there is the third level in which the communication is of the kind described in the last part of Essay 4. This, as I have been saying, does directly pertain to the substantive actuality of self-presence and, consequently, results in a real self-present We. It is this and only this sort of unity that I intend to call personal. With these distinctions in place, we can now turn our attention to the ontology of Who or Name.

CHART A

Consciousness-situations

c = conscious of
∉ = not conscious of

1.   (x∉y) · (y∉x)

2.   (x∉y) · (ycx)

3.   (xcy) · (ycx)

4.   xc(ycx) · [(ycx) · y∉(xcy)]

5.   [(xcy) · x∉(ycx)] · yc(xcy)

6.   xc(ycx) · yc(xcy)

7.   [xc yc(xcy)] · [y∉ xc(ycx)]

8.   [xc yc(xcy)] · [yc xc(ycx)]

CHART B

Pre-communication Mutual Presence
of Self-Presence (from one side)

c = conscious of
p = present to

```
                              x
                            xpx
                          (xpx)
                        (xpx)cy                    c  y
                        (xpx)cy                    c  y
                      (xpx)c(ypy)                  c (ypy)
                      (xpx)c(ypy)                  c (ypy)
                    (xpx)c (ypy)cx                 c (ypy)cx
                    (xpx)c (ypy)cx                 c (ypy)cx
                  (xpx)c (ypy)c(xpx)               c (ypy)c(xpx)
                  (xpx)c (ypy)c(xpx)               c (ypy)c(xpx)
               [(xpx)c (ypy)c (xpx) ]            c [(ypy)c (xpx)c(ypy) ]
               [(xpx)c (ypy)c (xpx) ]            c [(ypy)c (xpx)c(ypy) ]
             (xpx)c[(ypy)c (xpx)c(ypy) ]         c (ypy)c[(xpx)c (ypy)c(xpx) ]
             (xpx)c[(ypy)c (xpx)c(ypy) ]         c (ypy)c[(xpx)c (ypy)c(xpx) ]
           (xpx)c (ypy)c[(xpx)c (ypy)c(xpx) ]
```

34

ESSAY 6

NAME-CONSCIOUSNESS

The self-present subject is conscious of itself as being a person and as having or at least wanting to have a name. It is assured of the former simply in virtue of its awareness of the dignity or absolute worth of the form of self-presence as such. It is precisely because it is a person that it demands respect. In regard to the latter, however, it perceives that identity in any substantive sense can be achieved and maintained only in the We situation. In this essay, therefore, I wish to clarify the sense of person and the sense of name both in regard to one another and in regard to We.

The subject, because of the self-presence of its consciousness, has dignity. That is to say, it is of absolute worth and, consequently, deserves absolute respect. It is in virtue of its dignity that the subject is a person. All other reasons such as moral responsibility, capacity for ownership, etc., are only consequent upon this one fundamental source of personhood. Now there are three related observations to be made about the status of being a person. First, it is a given; it is discovered. It is not something I produce but rather it is a situation in which I find myself. I cannot, therefore, take any credit for being a person. Second, it is not a character that is distinctive of me, but rather is something shared in an identical way with all self-presences. Nothing in it or about it carries my signature. In a real sense, it is something other than me. And third, it directly extends to my whole substantial existence. The entire domain of my actuality has this dignity. There is no aspect or feature of my being that is excluded from participation in the absolute worth of my self-presence.

From these three observations it follows that I can do nothing to increase or diminish this dignity. It derives solely from the form of my being as a self-presence. The respect that it commands is, therefore, absolutely independent of any qualities I may produce in myself through my own actions and attitudes and its prohibition against the mere use of being extends to all, including myself, and yields to no exception. On the other hand, this absolute worth cannot provide my existence with those qualities, absolute or otherwise, that it can possess properly in virtue of their being mine. For example, I am not a good man because as man I have dignity. The character of my existence, as distinctly I, is and can be affected only by that the existence of which depends upon my knowing and willing. I am **self-present** whether I will it or not. Although I am indeed self-present and, therefore, in a sense this situation is mine, it is not mine in the fullest sense of being something for which I am responsible. I does not derive from nor bear upon the absolute uniqueness of my identity. It does not come out of any act by which the I is uniquely itself.

To be a person, therefore, pertains to the essence of the human being and indeed announces both the absolute worth of that essence and an equally absolute prohibition against its possessor ever being reduced by anyone (including himself) to the status of a mere thing for use. In other words, to be a person is to have an essence that commands unqualified respect. It is the essence of man rather than some action, attitude, or intention that definitively removes him from the world of things for mere use. Being a person, however, does not complete the proper perfection of the human being. In fact, it does not even provide the human being with its ultimate or greatest perfection. This ultimate completing perfection occurs only in the actuality of having a name or, more precisely at least for our purposes, in the actuality of being a name.

The indwelling of identification in We-consciousness accomplishes, as I have said, the subject's completion and the participation of its existence precisely as unique in absoluteness. This form or mode of existing gives the subject at least an inchoative satisfaction of its will to be in the fullest sense of that word. All of this, however, occurs in and indeed is a varied manifestation of the actuality of self-presences being interrelated precisely as self-presences. In other words, the reality of the interdependent relatedness is the actuality in which, by reason of its form, the subjects participate in the absolute or perfect mode of being. The fullest actuality of I, therefore, is to be related, and indeed to be related in a mutuality where form is the actuality of the relation and is also somehow absolute. To be in the fullest and richest sense of the word is to be related. It is to be related to, i.e., to have a name.

To have a name, however, in this sense involves being called that name by the other or recognized by the other in the We and the other to the We. It also involves, in a completing fashion, the answering to the name. All of this together constitutes the fullest explicitation into We consciousness of its reality in the order of identity. It constitutes also the fullest explication of the actuality, uniqueness, and relatedness that are the content of the name. We know who we are in the act of knowing who the other is. This knowing the name is being.

Name is an actuality of consciousness which occurs in an order of being totally other than the order of essence or what. The order of what is given, functional, and common. The order of name or who is that of a self-actualization by the subject (though not by the subject alone) the form of which opens out to absoluteness that is not given, functional, or common. There is a proximity of the form of indwelling to existence as absolute that is different from and greater than that of any finite what form or essence. This is why the perfect actualization of the former produces characteristics in the substantial existence of the subject that can never be produced by the perfect actualization of the latter. In other words, the form of who (name) is closer to existence as substantial and absolute than is the form of any finite what (definition). Full reality or authenticity occurs in and through the form of identification or indwelling and, due to the proximity of this form to existence itself, the subject of self-presence receives a participating similitude to subsistent existence. The actualization of this form is most like absolute being because in this situation the form comes closest to being identical with the act of which it is the form.

      The ontological order of who or name is, therefore, radically different from the order of what or essence both because it is self-actualizing rather than given and because it gives the subject's existence a participation in absoluteness precisely in regard to the uniqueness of its identity rather than the commonness of its humanity. All of this is ultimately accomplished through respect. Through this act my existence, not merely as mine but indeed precisely as me, participates in the absoluteness of the form which is respected. In other words, by my own deliberate act I actualize in myself the ontological peculiarity of this form. I not only <u>have</u> it, I <u>am</u> it. This act, as fully realistic, as indeed the ultimate realism, makes me, its agent, fully real. In short, the act of being personal gives the substantial existence of the agent an actuality that participates in the absoluteness of necessity, unity, truth (authenticity), goodness (holiness), beauty, and completeness proper to subsistent existence as such.

      Now one can see that the order of person and the order of name, although quite different, are nevertheless intrinsically related. Man, in virtue of his essence, is a person. He is not, however, merely in virtue of this essence, a name. He is a what; he is not yet a who. This does not, of course, mean that by his essence he is a thing. It does mean he does not yet have the actuality of a completed relation of absolute respect. We can say, therefore, that the essence of the human being contains a vocation. It contains a call to the individual human to make himself become something his essence cannot give him. It contains a call to the actuality of the full being or realism of absolute and effective respect for the absolute dignity of self-presence. It is a call to a realism of being that is as absolute as the respect one has for the absolute worth of the person. In brief, it is a call to be absolutely as an absolute substantial act of respect for the dignity of the person. It is a call to participate in the ultimate realism of absolute being itself.

ESSAY 7

THE INITIAL QUESTION

A.

I wish now to gather together four distinguishable considerations which both individually and collectively point to <u>the</u> fundamental ontological question. In this essay, the presentation of the question is merely initial because its formulation is only partial. In Essay 9 it will be raised again and there its formulation will be completed.

First, mind is a will to be. As intellectual consciousness, however, it has a sense of existence not simply as to be in this or that way but also as to exist as such. Mind as intellectual wants, therefore, not just to exist in this or that way but to be in the fullest strength of to exist as such. It wants to be fully. It wants to be absolutely and this will is itself absolute. Mind has, therefore, a connatural instinct for and interest in being as maximally real, in existing absolutely, at least so far as this is possible for it. Furthermore, this instinct and interest draw the mind immediately to the interpersonal situation of identification and indwelling. It seems that its most fundamental and urgent concern to exist fully can somehow be met satisfactorily in this situation. In the sane mature mind no other human interest can seriously compete for primacy of importance with deep personal love. The mind instinctively knows that somehow this <u>is</u> to be fully and completely. Somehow this is to exist absolutely. It would seem, therefore, that mind instinctively senses, however vaguely or obscurely, that the ultimate perfection of being occurs in and through the form of indwelling, i.e., the situation in which the existence of who or name is both constituted and maximized by the actual activity of identification with another who, and that this existence occurs in and is identical with the existence of a shared or common essence (or what). It is sensed, in other words, that this form is somehow the one that is most proper and intrinsic to existence itself. And in this form mind's interest is absolute.

The second consideration concerns the dignity of the person. Simply in virtue of its form of self-presence or essence, the human subject demands and rightly deserves absolute respect. The dignity of the self-consciousness mind requires unconditionally that, as such, it must not be used, computed, or otherwise treated as a thing. It is absolutely different from a thing. One must not take the posture of a detached uninvolved observer in its regard. And this fact is independent of everything else in the world including and especially the actions of the subject himself. There is, in other words, a peculiar absolute character to being in the order of person. The fundamental worth of the individual human precisely and exclusively in virtue of its humanity is presented to the mind as without limit or condition and totally unproduced. It is simply absolute and there.

The third consideration concerns a peculiar characteristic of being in the order of name. The determined unyielding will to treat the dignity of humanity in every individual with the absolute respect that it deserves and to allow no considerations of personal freedom or interest to qualify or manipulate that respect gives one's substantial existence precisely as who a character of holiness.

But what is this character? We certainly recognize it when we see it, but it is very difficult to analyze. It clearly points to something that has happened to the existence of the subject not insofar as it is human but precisely insofar as it is a name. It pertains to the existence I am by and in the very act of willing. It has to do with existence more precisely as me rather than as mine. Also it says much more than someone is good. The strength and absolutely uncompromising attitude of the will gives the subject's act of existence a fullness, intensity, and authenticity not normally expressed or meant simply by the word "good." Holiness or sanctity conveys such an existential veracity and a closeness by similitude to why being is in the first place that it takes on a necessity that shares in the necessity of existence itself. This is not only much more than goodness, it is also much more than dignity. This is to participate in the authority with which existence must be. Sanctity calls for more than the affection due to goodness and the respect due to dignity. It calls essentially and primarily for the reverence due to the absolute authority with which existence asserts that it must be, and only incidentally for admiration at the continued presence of such an attitude in a will that is ever free.

In other words, sanctity is the manifestation by participating similitude of the ultimate absolute total realness of existence. It is the character of an individual existence that is fully real, fully conformed with what it means to be. It is the clarity of an existence that is absolutely true to existence itself. In short, it is the character and clarity of the authenticity of existence being perfectly itself, of the truth of the integrity of an act of existence revealing the necessity by which the absolute radical good of existence must be.

The fourth and final consideration has to do with what might be called the existential ought. Existence expresses a radical intrinsic authority and law in regard to itself, namely, it ought to be. To be is good. And this goodness is the source of the authority and law for existence and, therefore, of an imperative dictating how existence is to be treated. The sane mind feels a connatural fraternal interest in helping things be. It also feels a prohibition against the stupid or the malicious destruction of anything however humble its existential status. And it is important to recognize that this prohibition is to be distinguished from those which are based on mind's respect for itself. Stupidity offends the dignity of mind and subverts its sanity; malice is the very non-being of mind. The prohibition I am talking about, however, originates in the dignity of the object. Everything that is, however otherwise insignificant, is in this one single respect deserving of our unqualified respect, namely, that it is. It may not, perhaps, attain to the absolute dignity of a person which constitutes an absolute prohibition against its mere use. Nevertheless, it does participate in the dignity of existence itself. Its willful abuse constitutes, therefore, a violation of this existential dignity and this violation carries with it the unavoidable penalty of at least some erosion, however small, of the foundation of the sanity of that faculty whose whole business is being.

Every act of existence asserts its goodness and its consequent imperative to be. In the case of the situation of identification, of indwelling, however, the existential imperative is absolute. The goodness of existing this way seems to be virtually identical with the goodness of existence as most fully actual, as most fully itself. In other words, the form of this situation is so perfectly fitted to the realizability of existence that it makes the situation participate in and reveal the absolute goodness of existence in itself. And the imperative expressed in its act of existence has, consequently, the fullest authority possible for an ought. It participates in the fundamental imperative by which being as such asserts that in virtue of its goodness it absolutely should be.

In other words, the form of indwelling by which similitude is mutually recognized with sympathetic openness to identification and in which dignity is shown a mutual absolute respect, so actualizes the possibility of existence that, at least in virtue of itself, it does not limit the act of existence. It is somehow identical with this act as such. In fact, it can be said that it is the primary connatural form of existence such that it is what it is to exist. To be this way is, at least in virtue of the form, to exist without qualification. In this case, therefore, the form fully possesses and expresses the unqualified goodness of being in itself. It consequently fully and perfectly expresses the ought of existence. This form should be just as existence itself should. And the ultimate certifying credential of the authenticity of this imperative is the absolute peace it produces in mind. This peace is the calm of a faculty of being that knows instinctively when it is at home. To be this way is, quite simply, to be, and the mind knows it.

Although these four considerations need to be distinguished, they are nevertheless intimately connected with one another, and I now want to clarify this connection. The point about which they all turn is the peculiar relation between the form of the completed situation of indwelling and the actualizability of existence. This relation would seem to be one of connaturality such that the form in question, in and of itself, perfectly fits existence. Unlike any other form, this one is so connected with existence itself that it is absolutely meant to be. And, on the other hand, the act of existing is absolutely meant to have this form. In other words, this form so conforms to existence as act that it is identical with it and does not in any way, of itself, limit the perfection of the act. Being with this form is, at least in virtue of the form, totally actual and, therefore, totally real.

Mind, as intellectual consciousness, is the faculty of being. Its whole interest and concern is reality. By its own peculiar nature, its own reality and sanity depend on the success of its act of finding and conforming to the real. It consequently has a connatural interest in the form of identification as offering it the possibility of absolute reality and sanity. Through this form, mind itself becomes perfectly actual and real.

The absolute worth of the self-present being that we call its dignity derives from the absolute perfection and goodness of the inchoative form of indwelling which is given to the subject in virtue of its essence. In this case, the worth is mediated through the real possibility for indwelling contained in the subject's self-presence. In other words, self-presence is the formal possibility of the perfection and goodness of indwelling, and it is this perfection and goodness that command absolute respect. It is the form of identification and its relation to existence, i.e., its reality, that is respected in self-presence as containing its possibility. Without this possibility, self-presence would be just another form in nature and could not command absolute respect. Only the absolutely real or its form command absolute respect for its worth.

Sanctity is that absolute authenticity of the being of a subject which it has through the realism of its unqualified act of respect for the dignity of self-presence. Through this act, which directly affects the character of its existence precisely as an identity, it affirms the goodness and worth of existence itself in the form of identification to be absolute. By the realism of this act in which it conforms all of its interests and possibilities to the worth of existence under this form, the subject makes itself absolutely real, it gives itself perfect integrity. Its existence precisely as who it is (rather than what it is) participates in the absolute actuality and realism of existence itself as formalized in identification.

Finally, the consideration of the existential ought turns directly on the relation between the form of indwelling and existence itself. Every ought of any kind derives ultimately from the absolute goodness of existence. Perhaps what I mean here can be best clarified through a distinction. It is obvious that the perfection of any thing is its greatest possible actualization. This is the sense in which it is. To be is the ultimate as well as fundamental perfection. Now it is appropriate for a thing to be perfect, that is to say, for it to be as actual as it can. The actuality of a thing is its good and, therefore, its perfection. It is in this sense that good is desirable.

This thrust or pull of a thing toward its good is _not_, however, what I mean by the existential ought. I mean that the goodness of existing possesses an authority to be fully, i.e., to be perfect. Existence, as good without qualification or condition, should be precisely because it is good for it to be. Therefore, I am saying that together with what could be called the attractiveness of existence there is also the imperative of existence. And this is what I mean by the existential ought.

Now the form of existence both modifies and participates in its actuality. And its participation is, of course, determined by the connaturality of its modification to the act of existence itself. For example, it is closer to what existence as an act is all about to be a human rather than to be a tree. In the former instance the act of existing suffers from less formal restriction than it does in the latter. In other words, in the form of humanity the existential act is more itself than it is in the form of a tree. It enjoys greater amplitude to be itself. Existence as such can be said, therefore, to be more comfortable, more at home, in the form of humanity than in the form of treeness.

It follows that the authority of the absolute goodness of existence is more compelling in the case of the act of existence of a human being than it is in the case of the act of existence of a tree. The greater closeness of the connaturality of the form of being human to the act of existence gives that form the greater capacity for announcing the authority of existence and for giving a particular act of existence greater participation in the authority of the goodness of to exist as such. In other words, the strength of the imperative to be of any particular act of existence will depend upon the proximity of its limiting or modifying form to what existence itself is all about.

B.

To return then to where I started. The form of the relationship of identification or indwelling seems to be so close to or even identical with what to exist is all about that it offers that act no resistance or restriction whatsoever. There is nothing further for existence to do. The perfection of the act of existence as such is to indwell. This is not perfection according to some limited and limiting form. This is the perfection of the act as such in and of itself that gives its appropriate form or, more precisely, is its appropriate form. So, in this case, we can say that such an act or, equivalently, such a form, ought to exist absolutely because it is absolutely good. The situation of identification absolutely ought to be.

There is, however, something very strange about all this. Every being and situation that I have met and that has carried the peculiar characteristic under our consideration has itself been totally frail and anything but absolute. The mind that pursues the absolute, the individual endowed with dignity, the one who achieves holiness, and the historically particular relation of identification, all are existentially frail. No being that I meet looks absolute in and of itself. And above all, the being that I myself am reveals to me no absolute foundation of its own. On the contrary, it reveals an almost total frailty. I clearly do not have to be. I am in a certain very real sense, a mere fact. I did not bring myself into existence. I do not know whether I could take myself totally out of existence, but I do know that I do not possess the resource to guarantee my continuance in existence.

This peculiarity raises the fundamental ontological question: how can this be so. Now this question about being has two sides. From the one side it may be asked how can these absolute features show up in the profiles of such fragil and unnecessary beings. From the other side it may be asked, if existence is in itself the way it has been described, how can it show up at all under such limitations and restrictions. In both cases the substance of the question is whether existence makes sense. Is there any being in which existence, as act and perfection, is totally itself, a being that simply is a subsistent act of existing, and to which all limited versions stand in some kind of relation of origin and similitude? This would seem to be the right ordering of the question because it is far more remarkable that the perfection of the act of existence should find itself in limiting situations than that it should be simply and perfectly itself.

This formulation leads to the question's following further specifications. Is there an original being whose essence is to exist and which is, therefore, the subsistent perfect goodness of existence? Such a being would, of course, possess an authority to exist that could suffer no restricting condition and, therefore, quite simply would have to be. It would be absolutely impossible for it not to exist. And if to be personal is, as such, being in the fullest sense of the word, would not this absolutely perfect and necessary act of existence have to be a consciousness whose total reality is to be personal, to be an act of identification, an indwelling? And if so, would not the whole reality of such a being consist in the actuality of who it is? Would not its total reality be its name. The ultimate ontological question would come, therefore, to this: <u>who</u> is that being whose essence is to exist and in relation to whom the community of finite beings enjoys a limited participatory similitude.

Mind's interest in this question is radical, vital, and absolute. Mind is an unconditional will to be. It is self-consciousness concerned for its existence. It is self-conscious existence concerned for itself. It is existence as an act of self-presence concerned to be. The will to be is, therefore, absolutely serious. It has the seriousness of being itself.

The primary essential business of mind is being. This statement must, of course, be deliberately and explicitly ambiguous. Mind is intelligence. As such, its concern, indeed its life, is conformity to being. This conformity is actually its own being. And therein, of course, lies the ambiguity. Mind's will to be must be translated into a concern for what is. Indeed, its presence to itself which constitutes its actuality is realized <u>in</u> its act of conforming. Its actuality as a self-presence depends, therefore, on its being true. Being true in relation to being, it is true in relation to itself, i.e., it is what it is and is supposed to be. The actualization of mind in regard to total reality is truth. Truth is its realization.

The pursuit of being is, therefore, the essential vital task of mind. In order to be fully as what it is, mind must know being. It is not enough, however, that it know this or that individual, or set of individuals, or even for that matter all the individuals in the community of items that limit their act of existing. The mind must, in its own ultimate interest, get at and grasp that which is absolutely connected with its concern, i.e., what it means to be. The mind's peculiarity is that to be mind is not merely to be this or that but, in this or that, to be. This is what it pursues and this is what it looks for in this or that. Only a grasp on what it means simply to be, therefore, offers mind the opportunity to have a sense of the lay of the field of reality and a sense of its own real prospects. Recognizing and dealing with the question of what to exist is all about is the mind's necessary exploratory act on the way to self-actualization.

The result of this exploratory act, however, as important as it is for the ultimate interest of mind, cannot by its nature provide this interest with its perfect satisfaction. To understand or grasp what it means to be is knowing <u>about</u> being; it is not an immediate relating <u>to</u> being. Being, in the proper and fullest sense, is substance. It is, therefore, only in a real relation to an actual substance that mind can fully actualize itself.

To know what it means to be cannot, at least by itself, be the ultimate purpose and final perfection of the mind. It can be and, in fact, is that necessary move by which mind discovers whether there does indeed exist a substance, a being in that fullest sense, in relation to which it can achieve its fullest actualization as the act of being true.

The answer and its question, that is to say, speculation, theorizing, and knowledge <u>about</u> being, cannot be the ultimate end of mind. Only that in relation to which it can achieve the realization of itself as a name, as a who, through knowing as identification can be this end. It is only in being true to, and not merely in being true, that mind makes itself fully real. This question is, therefore, as I have said, an exploratory act. It is not mere thinking about; it is a looking for. It is the ultimate expression of mind precisely as a look, a look expecting both to find and to be recognized. It is only in this sense that the question is vital, absolutely serious, totally important.

Another curious though critically important thing about this ontological question is that if it is to be given an answer that can satisfy mind's ultimate vital interest, it must be asked in a different mode. It cannot in its speculative form, in which the asker positions himself as an observer at a detached and safe distance from the answer, receive a response that can effect the mind's substantial existence. To be effective, the question must be asked in the same mode of reality as that belonging to the being from which an answer is expected. It must be asked in the form: <u>who are you</u>. The response to the question in this form can never be mere information. The answer must be not merely the name of the answerer, but the name precisely as containing the answerer. It must be a communication in which the speaker is the message. The exchange must occur on the level of identification and indwelling. In other words, the question must be a personal request expecting a personal response. It is in this sense that the question and its answer become a substantial existential event generative of We.

Here, at least for the moment, thinking is at an end because it has completed the first stage of its work for mind. It has brought mind up to that for which all its deepest vital interests and instincts have been looking. Now something else must be done and something else must happen before thinking can resume its progress along the road of ontological understanding. Mind must relate to this being. It must identify with it by name, as who it is. Then it can move along in pursuit of deeper and richer understanding. If, however, mind stops and backs away, it inevitably trivializes both its search and itself. It places the very faculty of thought itself in the absurd position of doubting the ultimate worth of thinking except, perhaps, as a means of entertainment or as a way of distracting itself from the grim futility of its deepest interests and aspirations. In short, the refusal to go ahead turns thinking in on mind itself in such a way as to threaten its rationality and sanity.

C.

With these considerations in place, we now turn to the ontological question. First, is there a being whose mode of existence is identical with its act of existence such that no limit is placed upon that act's perfection precisely as existing? In other words, is there a being whose actuality is perfectly extensive with the full reality of to exist? And second, if so, who is it? What is its name?

In regard to the first part of the question, I offer the following response. Mind has an essential need for things to make sense. If they do not, or when it thinks they do not, it is threatened with madness. Precisely because mind is existence present to itself, the suspicion of existence as unintelligible becomes existence conscious of itself as non-being or mind as non-mind. The root of this danger is, of course, mind's connaturality with existence in which and through which it knows at the deepest level of self-consciousness that to exist is indeed intelligible. Therefore, only at the price of its own being can mind seriously entertain and encourage the attitude that existence is absurd. Truth is the actuality of mind and is mind's own intelligibility. For mind to convince itself, or attempt to do so, that existence is unintelligible is, therefore, unavoidably to destroy the necessary condition of its relation to itself. In this case, unlike that of other objects whose situation remains untouched by what we think, such a conviction is itself productive of its object. A mind convinced of its unintelligibility <u>is</u> unintelligible. This is the destruction of sanity precisely because it must begin with mind lying to itself in the clear light of its own connatural better judgment and thereby destroying itself as the faculty of truth. The relation of mind present to itself then becomes a nightmare.

Now it makes no sense whatever that the perfection of existence, especially as revealed in the characters of necessity and absoluteness proper to dignity, sanctity, and identification as described above, might adequately be explained by the limited fragil beings in which we discover it. It is ridiculous to think that such perfection should have its ultimate foundation in beings whose distinctive ontological signature is precisely that their essences record nothing necessary or absolute in regard to their own existences. In other words, such beings and indeed the entire community of such beings (actual and possible) is totally devoid of any capacity for explaining the reality of this perfection. They cannot on their own resource clarify either the sheer possibility of such perfection in the first place nor how it comes to find itself in unnecessary limited beings. Perfection cannot ultimately have its origin in nothing nor can it negate itself by being its own limit.

Clearly then then, the perfection of existence makes sense because in some order of reality it is authentically itself, that is to say, it is necessary, absolute, and unlimited. In some order of reality, existence is fully and authentically itself. However, only that which subsists is properly and in the full sense of the word is a being. And that which in its consciousness of its existence and in its presence to itself possesses itself and dwells in itself most properly subsists. Existence at its best and truest to itself is, therefore, mind. And, as we have seen, mind at its best is being personal, is in the relation of identification. Consequently, the perfection of existence is fully and authentically itself in a subsistent act of presence and identification, of being personal. In other words, there is a being whose entire reality is its act of existing, who is, therefore, subsistently good, who consequently absolutely must be and, of course, must be with the full unlimited perfection of existence, whose whole actuality is the attitude or look of mind being personal and, therefore, in its self-presence is subsistently holy and true.

   Being in its completed picture is totally intelligible, and mind is or can be at home and at peace with reality. Everything in the world, to the extent that it exists, is a limited likeness of a being whose act of existence is its whole reality. And everything that exists, however humble, has some dignity and possesses some authority to be and to be itself because, as existing, it is a limited likeness of the subsistent goodness of that being and enjoys some limited participation in the authority and necessity with which it exists. Our humanity, furthermore, in its dignity reveals a potential for existing in a way and with a scope that comes very close to what existence at its best is all about and, therefore, in a limited manner participates through this likeness in the absolute character of that being. Finally, the realism of the firm and determined will to respect at all costs this dignity, together with the peculiar relation between the form of identification and existence itself, gives the otherwise frail individual an existential authenticity and necessity that are a clear and remarkably close likeness of the truth and holiness of this being. Fragil, limited, and unnecessary individuals, by being personal, act out a portrait of that being whose entire reality is this attitude, and in so doing, participate by similitude in its necessity and absoluteness. In short, they become holy.

I now turn to the second part of the ontological question: who is this being; what is his name. An attempt to answer this question must begin by getting clear exactly what it is asking for. And this can best be done by examining the question in its natural environment. Its most vital situation is that of one person asking another: <u>who are you</u> or <u>what is your name</u>. All other situations are derivative. In this scene, it is, of course, absolutely clear what I am not asking for. I do not want to know if the individual exists, nor do I want to know what kind of thing it is. And lastly, except in the most trivial formal situations, I am not trying to find out what the individual is called, i.e., what his verbal tag may be. When I ask this question, I am looking for something that, whatever else it may be, is not information. Precisely what, then, could possibly suffice as a real and satisfactory answer to this question?

First, the question itself assumes the existence of something to which the asker does not and cannot have access simply through investigation. I do not need someone to tell me either what it means for him to be human or what he is called by other people. This much I can get from other people with or without his knowledge and consent. Therefore, when I ask him "who are you" I am looking for a name as containing something <u>only</u> this individual can give me because it is something to which <u>only</u> he has immediate and original access. I am looking for a name whose meaning is not the use that others may make of it, but rather whose content is his act of answering both as act and precisely as his. In this case, the act of responding contains and communicates the uniqueness and the self-consciousness of the uniqueness of the actuality of the respondent's own relation of self-presence. Through his act of answering in which he conveys the sign or symbol of the unique actuality he is and is conscious of being as self-presence I am given access to the respondent's own self as his indwelling.

Clearly this is a complex nondiagramatic event of acting and knowing in a domain of reality very different from that of essences and understanding. The name in this sense expresses the uniqueness of the existence of the form of the relation of the other's self-presence as actualized in its relating to me in my capacity as a formally identical self-presence relating to him through the act of my question. In other words, this total event is comprised of the interdependent actions of relating through "asking who" and "giving the name" as sustaining the actuality of the individual self-presences. It is that vital moment in which through the completion of the actualization of the whole form of personality the subjects maximize the actuality of their uniqueness as names. This is the actualization of the whole form of identification.

In the light of these considerations it can now be seen that at the center of the name-asking and name-giving event is the actualization of that form which is most connatural to existence and which gives existence the greatest amplitude to be itself. In this event, knowing as "I know you" is not understanding. It is not a getting at the universal form in the individual, but rather a becoming one with the individual the actuality of the uniqueness of whose relation of self-presence is being maximized in the developing unity contained in the complete form of being personal. This is knowing in its most perfect form because the known is in the knower through an indwelling in the actuality of a relationship of identification. This is the most perfect knowing because the subsistent reality itself is grasped immediately and precisely in the uniqueness of its self-conscious individuality. The sense of the name is inconceivable. In this knowing, unlike any other, the very substantial existence of the knower becomes true and good. This is being becoming most itself as subsistent, and doing so in the act of being in relation to the act of its existence in and through its act of being in relation to another self.

D.

With these thoughts in place it should now be clear that there is a primacy of who over what, i.e., of personal name over essence. Identity as self-presence in the act of identification with the other is the most perfect mode of substantial unity and, therefore, of being. The possessor and the subsisting identity are more perfectly being than merely that which is possessed and in which the identity subsists. In other words, there is a primacy of the personal mode of being over the essential mode because the form of the complex relation of being personal is closer to, more connatural with, and gives greater amplitude to the perfection of the act of existing than does the finite essential mode. The former mode allows this act to be most authentically itself, i.e., holy and clear. Also, the act of personal knowing, the act of knowing the other, enjoys an absolute primacy over any other kind knowing both because of the immediacy and completeness with which it unites the knower and the known and because of the effect it has on the substantial existence of the knower.

Given this priority, therefore, it follows that the ultimate essential interest of the human mind must make the answer to the question "who are you" when directed to that being whose essence is to exist the ultimate objective of its entire investigative effort. If one can have this answer given in the vital primary way described above, there opens up the prospect of the perfect satisfaction of mind's every existential interest through some sort of participation in that being's personal and essential modes of existence.

Who then is this being? His essential name is, of course, "He who is," *Qui* *est*. This is his most proper name because, as such, it does not signify merely some form but rather his very act of existing itself. And since this act of existing is his essence, is what he is, and since this is uniquely so for him, "He who is" is most properly his name. It both meaningfully and exclusively signifies his being. All other essential names which, indeed, may quite properly be his are contained in this one since the deepest and richest perfection signified by any and every essential name is "to exist."

  Now, although this is an essential name, it nevertheless uniquely designates an intellectual being. Also, although this name is _per se_ public, it is nevertheless given to the community of other intellectual beings through its revelation in the existence of the members of the community of finite realities. Consequently, it can be the basis of a personal relation. Because mind understands that this being is subsistently and without any limit that which is most perfectly, authentically, and intimately best about itself, i.e., self-conscious existence, existence at its best, it sees a ground for the most perfect relation of identification of which it is capable. In this case, I can identify with that being which, precisely because it is existential perfection without limit, is that in regard to which the perfect in me stands in a transcendent similitude it cannot have to any finite being. In this relationship, one achieves an actualization that transcends absolutely any that might be possible in a relationship with another finite subject. Here the subject is most at home both with the other and with itself because the indwelling is with that being who is subsistently what I am all about. I see me more in the other than I do in myself because the other, in this case, is subsistently and without limit and, indeed, originally that which is the limited best in me, i.e., existence. This is a most peculiar kind of recognition in which one sees not merely a likeness and not merely a source, but a resemblance that in a sense is more authentically like me than I am. This relationship is the environment of mind's fullest possible actuality as self-presence. The name that it achieves in this relationship is a function of the name of the being to which it is related, i.e., "to be." And this identity manifests itself in the same mode as does the identity of Qui est, i.e., as holy and true.

"He who is," as the subsistent act of existing and, so, as the subsistent fullest perfection of existing, must be subsistent mind in its act of self-presence. Finite mind, on the other hand, is attracted to this subsistent perfection because its own reality is a participation by likeness in the reality of this perfection, and in a relation of identification its personal knowing of this mind would give it a transcendent insight into its own perfection from the point of view of that perfection as it exists subsistently and without limit. In other words, finite mind could then view itself in the clearest possible perspective, i.e., from the viewpoint of the subsistent reality of which it is a limited likeness. This insight would, in turn, enable it to actualize its self-presence to a degree otherwise absolutely beyond its reach, and, in fact, this insight would effect that transcendent actualization. In this situation it would have the most real identity and the most significant name possible to it through a relation to that being whose essence is to exist and based on its essential name Qui est.

These considerations, however, lead now to two crucial and intimately connected vital problems. In the situation of identification and indwelling, the mind's will to be becomes the will to see and possess the other or to possess the other through seeing. In any case, the actuality of mind as intellect consists in the act of seeing into reality. Now the first problem is this: although mind knows that there exists a being whose act of existing is its essence, it does not meet and touch that existence nor directly see into it as essence. Everything here happens by a kind of frustrating indirection. The whole vital thrust of mind to be draws it inexorably and with increasing intensity and single-mindedness to this being as the full subsistent intelligibility of all existence and, therefore, the ultimate uniquely proper and actualizing object of intellect as such. Indeed, the more perfect mind's relation of identification with this being becomes, the more actual mind itself becomes and, in turn, the more attractive this being becomes. Nevertheless, even when mind has matured to the point where it understands that its will to be is indeed equivalently the will to see this being, it finds that it does not see it and cannot discover any clear route along which by its own determination and resource it can certainly come to see it.

The second problem originates in our perception of what seems to be the form of personality and interpersonal relating. In this regard, it seems that personal identity, whatever else it may involve, is basically a self-conscious real relation to another real identity. Without this relation, a subject is a name only in some rudimentary sense. In other words, the form of full and perfect personality would seem to require this personal relating. One's personal name, therefore, in the sense I have been talking about it, would seem to depend absolutely upon this relation for its real sense. Furthermore, this investigation indicates that this form enjoys a peculiar status, at least for finite beings, as being both more connatural to the act of existence and as not being reducible to, predicated of, or derived from essence.

In the light of this peculiar status, therefore, it would be natural for the human mind to wonder whether behind the essential name "He who is" there might not be another name, or names. Is it possible that although in this being the essential name is unique and, therefore, can be the basis of a personal relationship for us, there may be other names, identities, that are absolutely irreducible to this essential name? Is it possible that behind this *per se* public name there may be absolutely private names signifying identities that are totally personal and constituting an interpersonal life which is totally hidden and whose privacy cannot be invaded? Finally, is it possible that, at least for the human mind, to view this being through the form of personality according to which we would think of it as several really different identities existing in the perfect relationship of identification, i.e., subsisting in their one existential act of being to one another, might provide an opportunity not available through the form of the essential name? In other words, is there a possibility of considering the existence of this being as the subsistent perfection of the form of personality as well as that of essence and in this way achieving a mode of knowing that makes possible an identification that cannot be achieved through the essential name?

Now this being, as the unlimited subsistent act of self-presence, or as that act of existing which is identical with its form of self-presence must, of course, be both personal and existentially simple. Nevertheless, it remains conceivable that it might also be, without compromising this simplicity, relationally and personally complex. In fact, as I have said, the peculiar relation of the complex form of personality to the amplitude of the perfection of existence in finite reality justifies the consideration that in the unlimited reality this form might also be found, although obviously in its ultimate actualization. This, however, would seem to be as far as theoretical mind can get. What this form would be positively like in its ultimate actualization seems to lie beyond the reach of a mind whose speculative understanding is confined within the limits of its own mode of existing. Furthermore, even if speculative reflection could decide this matter it could never tell us who these identities are because personal names cannot be found out in this way.

These two problems reduce, then, to questions of access. I do not find that by my own resource I have intuitive access to the existence and essence of "He who is," and it would also seem that I have no access through my own resource to his purely personal or proper name, if indeed he even has such a name. And, as I have said, these two problems are intimately connected. First, they are both rooted in the human mind's perception of the relation between its ultimate interest in being and the existential primacy of the form of personality. Second, in regard to their solution, if indeed they have a solution, it may be the case, that in virtue of the existential primacy of who over what that in "He who is" the identities and their sustaining interrelations are in their form so perfectly the ultimate intelligibility of existence that, through interpersonal identification and indwelling with these identities, one could begin to so participate in this form and the primacy of its connatural fit to existence that one's mind would also begin to participate in their ability to see this existence and essence. In other words, the interpersonal knowing of these identities might lead by participating similitude in the order of who, by being a member of the family or being a relative, to a participating connaturalization of the mind's ability to see that existence and essence which properly belong to these identities.

These speculations, then, bring mind up to either the ultimate limit or the ultimate condition of the fulfillment of its will to be. If there are no interpersonally relating identities, or if there are but their names must remain permanently secret, and if as a consequence, vision in the sense I mentioned is also permanently out of the question, then one is left to wonder whether mind's will to be may not be ultimately absurd. On the other hand, if one leaves room for the opposite alternative, the practical questions then become the following. Under what sort of circumstance might one expect to be given the name or names, and how could one certify the authenticity of the message. In regard to the first question, it is not clear to me that an answer can be provided through speculative reflection. In regard to the second, it would seem that the distinctive existential character of "He who is," i.e., absolute existential authenticity or holiness and truth would have to signature the event. In other words, it would have to be clear that the message is true because its original communicator is his act of existence and is, therefore, subsistent absolute goodness. In short, the sanctity of the communication would have to certify that both the communicator and the message are the truth, prima veritas.

Here, then, is the mind's outer speculative reach in regard to the possibility of the satisfaction of its will to be fully according to the most perfect mode of existence it can discover. It can get no further without the occurrence of an event over which it has no control if, indeed, such an event is even possible. This is my response to the "Ontological Question" in its initial formulation. Before moving to the question in its ultimate formulation I wish to give some consideration to what is really the anti-being of subject, i.e., alienation.

ESSAY 8

ALIENATION

A.

My interest here is quite deliberately narrow. I merely want to throw more light on the preceding considerations by examining what happens when a personal relationship is destroyed and what might be the cause of this destruction. We will, therefore, inspect how this is done, what are its consequences, and three unrealistic judgments that inevitably lead to it.

Personal relationships are destroyed either because they were ill-advised in the first place and simply disintegrate under the force of internal and external pressures or because someone wants a return of his freedom. Actually, even in the former situation, it is freedom that has become the critical issue. The essential destructive act is, therefore, infidelity. The usual attendent act is deception. At least for a time, it is normal for there to be an attempt to conceal the infidelity.

The destructive act is in itself quite simple. Its consequences, however, are as negatively complex as that which is destroyed. The first and most immediate consequence is the termination of the identities established in the relationship. Who I was, the name I had, is over. This is why alienation seems like death. It is death. Who I was is dead.

The second consequence occurs in the subjectivity and self-presence of the agent of the alienation. Just as the relating activity of the subject actualizes the relation of self-presence which exists according to its modes of knowing and will, so the destructive activity of alienation weakens this relation. It literally deactualizes the subject. Just as the form of personality provides the greatest amplitude for the perfection of existence through its connaturality with existence so the form of alienation maximally negates the perfection of existence through its radical incompatibility with being. It is, indeed, the proper form for the annihilation of the perfection of existence. Consequently, just as the form of personality maximizes the authenticity of existence as holiness and truth, so the form of alienation maximizes anti-existence as evil and lie. This constitutes, of course, the maximal trivialization of the subject as an individual and the destruction of the personal aspect of its relation to itself. In other words, just as the form of fidelity is intrinsically holy because of its proximity to and connaturality with existence as such so the form of infidelity is intrinsically evil because of its destructive incompatibility with the perfection of existence. It is also intrinsically ugly because it is the deformation of existence. Alienation is the suicide of the subject as a self-presence and as a self-consciously significant identity.

The third consequence also occurs in the subjectivity of the agent. In the human mind there is a vital movement toward a harmonious unity between attitudes and insights such that any serious tension or conflict between them will sooner or later be resolved in favor of one or the other. We will either change the attitude or subvert the insight through calculated doubt. This is particularly true where the insight involves a limit on freedom. For example, if one is determined to do something he clearly feels to be wrong he will eventually find reasons to doubt the reliability of the feeling and thereby eliminate it as an influence.

Now, in the alienating act, one negates the dignity of the other. It is essentially an act of disrespect. One has access to this dignity, however, through a feeling about self-presence as such.

It is through this feeling that mind detects the absolute worth of existence itself as manifest in a being that in virtue of its humanity is capable of the form of personality. This intuitive awareness is, however, absolutely incompatible with the alienating attitude which would reduce the other to the status of a thing for mere use, i.e., to the status of an object that can impose no limit on my freedom in its regard. Consequently, the harmonic unity of mind will inevitably move it to produce reasons that remove the conflict by suppressing the intuition in a cloud of doubt. One deliberately blinds the mind so that it cannot see.

The inevitable result of this act is a living trap. The alienating agent remains a being of needs that cannot be met in any situation other than the interpersonal relationship. But blindness to the dignity of self-presence makes a successful involvement in such a relationship absolutely impossible. The agent can see neither his own nor the other's reality to which he must relate. And without vision the mind has no way of changing its attitudes. The alienating agent is thereby confirmed in his own alienation.

We can move now to a consideration of three attitudes that initiate the process of alienation. Each of these derives from a fundamental mistake about reality that need not and, indeed, should not be made. Each of these attitudes is, therefore, in its own way an exercise in stupidity.

B.

The first attitude is that love is omnipotent. It is the view that love can overcome all difficulties merely by the force of its own intensity. This leads, of course, to the suspension of that prudential judgment required at the initial stage of a relationship to determine its real possibility in the face of those serious practical difficulties that can reasonably be expected to arise given the individuals and their probable futures.

If one thinks that a human relationship can exist merely in the order of the intersubjective without also and necessarily existing in the world of things, one easily believes that it can be produced and sustained by love independently of practical intelligence. This leaves the subject susceptible to involvements that have no chance of long-term success. It also makes otherwise potentially important relationships vulnerable to internal and external pressures that could have been either avoided or minimized and which cumulatively over time can overpower the relationship. Realism, therefore, requires the exercise of prudential intelligence as an essential component of the interpersonal relationship.

We may usefully though perhaps somewhat artificially distinguish three classes of such prudential judgments. The first concerns the sense of the frailty of the human condition. To attempt at a serious relationship with a person who drinks too much, drives foolishly, smokes heavily, or who in general is simply indifferent to the ordinary requirements of maintaining one's health, would be inviting a disaster in one's personal life.

The second concerns the compatibility of what might be called "life styles." If, for example, the professional interests and situations of the parties are such as to make a common life style virtually impossible without an extraordinary sacrifice on the part of one person, it would be stupid not to see this prospect as a very high risk. Deep seated interests normally cannot be suppressed indefinitely.

The last concerns the sensitivity to and seriousness about the needs that originate in self-presence. It is hardly an exaggeration to say that to attempt a serious relationship with someone who is childish about these kinds of matters is to virtually guarantee that one will miss the stable actualization of one's own subject in time.

Now these prudential concerns are critically urgent because, as I have already said, the individual lives in a time that has shape and, therefore, it is altogether possible that the consequences of imprudence may so alter the range of one's real options for action that, at some point in time, a trap may close. There may no longer exist any significant options for meeting one's most fundamental needs as a subject. In other words, one has irreversibly ruined one's life.

C.

The second attitude is a determination to have, so far as it is possible, unlimited freedom. It is the firm will to tolerate no restriction of freedom if the restriction can in any way be circumvented. There is, however, regardless of the subject's attitude and determination one limitation it can never circumvent, and that is its limitation by the needs that arise from subjectivity. No one can be free of this limit, at least no one who is sane.

The will to total freedom, therefore, inevitably initiates a dialectic. On the one hand, this will needs and wants the satisfaction of interests that by their very nature can be met only in an interpersonal relationship which, in its turn, is possible only through commitment and fidelity. On the other hand, it wants a totality of freedom that makes commitment impossible. If this attitude is inserted into an interpersonal relationship, it must inevitably destroy that relation. Each subject needs to have its fundamental interest in its own actualization satisfied with stability in time. The shape of time makes this necessity urgent. Furthermore, one's self-respect will not tolerate the known unbalanced situation in which one provides this stability for another person through commitment and serious investment of freedom but is not guaranteed such stability in return through the other's commitment. No person will permit themselves to be reduced to the status of a mere thing for the use of someone else.

Now since the will to total freedom must take this fact into account in its pursuit of the satisfaction of its needs without limiting freedom, it must employ deception. It must employ the language of deceitful ambiguity and concealment. Its language must be sufficiently true to elicit belief and deceitful enough to conceal the absence of commitment. This might be called the logic of use. It seems to me, however, that the human mind in regard to its most vital interest is intuitively infallible. It is in possession of an eventually unerring sense for the tone and feel of truth. It quite simply cannot be deceived indefinitely in such matters. Eventually, the sense of not being at home in the relationship and of not being at ease in the conversation, the feel of a wobble in its relation to itself, the sense of a name that is slipping away, the occasional dimming of its sense of actuality in the relationship, must force to the front of the mind's attention the vital question: what am I doing here.

All of this can, of course, surface initially as guilt. The similarity between the disintegration of one's identity as the agent of alienation and the disintegration of one's identity as the victim is sufficient to temporarily confuse. The subject seriously committed to another would strongly resist doubting the other since that act always appears to be destructive. Hence guilt. This is, of course, a temporary vulnerability to which the will to total freedom easily and instinctively plays. But eventually, the mind's sense of truth will force it, even after losing every argument, to recognize that the other is a liar. Freedom without limit is incompatible with truth. Eventually it must offend mind's sense of reality. The emotional reaction to being treated as a thing for mere use is hatred. The inevitable conclusion of the logic of use must be an emotional reaction which denies the other access and forces the dissolution of even the illusion of a relationship.

The will to total freedom derives from a fundamentally mistaken judgment about freedom.

Freedom subject to no law or restraint is a fictional illusion rooted in and generated by the self-idolatry of mind. It is the self-induced illusion of absoluteness minus necessity. That is why it is an ontological fiction. In effect, it is the idea of existence as absolutely trivial which is, of course, radically incompatible with and, indeed, hostile to the idea of existence as necessary because it is good. In a literal sense, it is the absurd notion of the being of anti-being or, from another perspective, mind as anti-mind. This is not simply the finite declaring itself to be infinite. This is being declaring itself to be subject to no necessity and, therefore, anti-being.

The will to total freedom is radical absolute evil because it is being in the very actuality of its presence to itself actively negating what it means to exist. That is to say, it is the negation of that necessity with which there must be existence because it is good as such and without qualification and, therefore, also of that necessity by which mind must recognize and respect this goodness. It is being using its very actuality to make itself a nonentity by willing itself to be totally and in every respect independent of all and any necessity. In short, the will to total freedom is the form of evil as such. It is, therefore, radically incompatible with and hostile to the form of personality. This form expresses connaturally the absolute goodness of existence in the fullest amplitude of its perfection and, therefore, contains the law of respect binding every mind and the possibility of authenticity and holiness for every mind that conforms to this law. It is precisely to this law that the will to total freedom stands in complete and total opposition. And that is why the form of such a will is the form of <u>per se</u> opposition to good. This is why it is <u>in itself</u> the form of evil.

Freedom is the mode of the agency of self-presence. It is that act **as** self-present, as mine and as me. In this sense the act is nondiagrammatic and, consequently, cannot be grasped through a diagrammatic use of concepts. It properly belongs to the order of the form of personality and cannot be seen through the perspective of essence.

Freedom is the mode of the perfect authentication of act as existence by and through it the act is totally itself owing none of its determinations to anything other than itself. This is existence in the fullest sense of actively and self-presently being itself. In this mode, consciousness gives itself the law of reality, of being real, which is the proper form of this act because of its (the form's) connaturality to existence. This is the law of respect for the absolute worth or dignity of existence. In other words, being as self-conscious announces to itself the proper form of reality so that, through the act of accepting this form, being makes itself real. Being as self-realizing in this sense is the ultimate authenticity. Being, therefore, as recognizing and accepting the law of respect for the dignity of existence and its authority, as good, to be, especially as at its best in the form of personality, is authentic existence. Freedom, in this sense, is the self-personalization and maximal realization of existence by the self-present act of respect. Freedom is, therefore, the mode of act as holy.

Perfect freedom is the mode of perfect act because it is the mode of perfect actualization of being in relation to itself. It is, indeed, the mode of being as self-relation as such. It belongs, therefore, to the form of personality rather than essence. In fact, the form of personality is actualized precisely through this mode of existence as act. Given the existential primacy of the form of personality, it follows that freedom is the mode of existence at its best, the mode of the perfection of existence in its fullest amplitude as self-relation in the form of personality, the mode of the sanctification of the act of existence in respect, and in the same conformity to the law of reality which mind precisely as self-conscious being gives itself, the mode of the ultimate authentication of the act of existence as truth. Finally, at least from the perspective of his being his act of relation to himself, it can be said that "He who is" is "to be free."

In the light of these considerations, it should be clear why the will to total freedom is radical ontological evil. Mind is being precisely as actualized in an act of self-presence. In this act it self-consciously announces to itself its absolute worth or dignity and its absolute authority to be as the imperative of its goodness. In other words, mind's consciousness of itself is its actuality and, as such, must involve the consciousness of its worth and authority. Indeed, precisely as self-consciousness, this awareness of worth and authority is the actuality of both. Now the mode of this act precisely as self-actuality is freedom. The complete realization of being consists, therefore, in the freedom of the self-present act by which it sets its attitude of respect for its perfection as existing. This makes the goodness of the being in which the goodness and authority of existence are announced absolutely authentic or holy. That is to say, being authenticates itself and so makes itself maximally actual in the free attitude of respect for the good and the authority of existence as absolutes.

If, however, mind, in an act of self-idolatry, asserts that its freedom is the absolute it makes itself in its very act of self-presence a liar. In that act it announces to itself that there is no good and no authority superior to the mode of freedom. Now just as real being as self-present in its mode of freedom is a complex act in self-consciousness in which the goodness and authority of the act of existing are both announced with absolutely evident truth and regarded with total respect and by which this very being makes itself a conformation of this announcement, so unreal being is a complex act in self-consciousness in which mind declares that its mode of existing is the ultimate value and in which it translates its will to be into the will to be absolutely free. Since, however, it is the act of existing that is the ultimate good and authority without which and apart from which there is no worth or dignity, this act in effect declares just that, namely, that there is no good or authority at all that is absolute and that, therefore, the only proper attitude toward being is contempt. Indeed, contempt is the signature of the will to total freedom.

Such a mind, by this act, makes itself radically evil. It is a self-conscious denial of good as such and a posture of contempt for being's competence to limit freedom. The immediate irony, however, is that due to the inescapable law of self-actualization in self-presence, such a mind makes itself to be that which it claims being to be, i.e., worthless. The act, precisely as his act, is absurd. The will to total freedom makes the mind a depersonalized liar, ontologically evil, and objectively contemptable. The ultimate irony, of course, is that this will constitutes a direct threat to the practical freedom of everyone else since it must view them as mere instruments for the pursuit of its own interests. Such a will cannot recognize any claim to a worth independent of its own interests and, as being established in the very fact of existence, constituting a practical limit to its freedom. In short, the will to total freedom is, in effect, the will to total use. This is the will to total power, the germ of totalitarianism, and the mortal enemy of our humanity.

At bottom, therefore, the will to total freedom is a confused and misdirected attempt on the part of the subject to satisfy its necessary vital interest in the absolute. The subject in the very substance of its relation to itself has needs that it wants met not only in a stable manner that accounts for time and its shape, but also definitively in a way that accounts for its sense of being more than time. It wants to be perfectly stable in its actuality, and this it can accomplish only in relation to an existential absolute. The confusion and misdirection arise when the will to be translates itself into the will to be an absolute. For a being of needs, this is self-idolatry that, as I have tried to show, inevitably produces a result the exact opposite of the one desired.

As I have also tried to show, however, the mind's interest in the absolute derives from its own structure. Mind is a self-conscious will to be. Because in this will it understands "to be" as such, it must see that to be, in the fullest and best situation that is proper to it, is to be absolutely. Because in this will it is self-present and, therefore, both the will to be and the understanding of to be are essential to the very act of its self-presence and subjectivity, it is an interest in the absolute. In other words, the actuality of the relation of self-presence is an interest in the absolute. Furthermore, and ultimately, the mode of existence as an act of self-presence, as indwelling, as existence as an act of act encompassing itself, is absolute in its mode. The form of personality, even in this inchoative stage, by reason of its connaturality to existence is, as I have said, absolute. Nevertheless, this very same act of self-consciousness is a clear awareness that its own very actuality is indeed anything but absolute. And herein precisely is the root of the anomaly of man: he is a being whose mode and form of the act of his self-presence is indeed absolute and yet the act of which it is the form is itself totally fragile and contingent. This, therefore, is also the root of the mind's confused pursuit of the illusion of total freedom in which it tries to satisfy its inescapable interest in the absolute by attempting to become that which it can never be, i.e., an existential absolute.

D.

This anomaly is also the source of the third attitude I wish to consider. I refer to that by which one tries to satisfy this interest through the expectation that another human being can and indeed should be his finality. That is to say, one expects the other to play the role of the existential absolute in which his needs can find their definitive satisfaction. This, of course, together with the first attitude, may be called "the romantic fallacy" and like the first attitude originates in a mistaken judgment about the relation of love to human limitations. In this case it is believed and expected that love is omnipotent and that it can so transcend the human condition that it can become or at least produce the equivalent of an existential absolute. This, however, for reasons we have seen is totally impossible. I am a being by participation. I am not a being whose essence is its existence. And about this fundamental situation I can do nothing. No matter how much one loves another he can never be that for another which he cannot be in and for himself. He cannot provide that definitive existential stability for another which he cannot out of his own resources provide for himself.

If, however, an interpersonal relationship matures as it should, it moves toward mutual clarity. This is the familiarity of identification, the openness of the self-consciousness of "We." But it is precisely in this clarity that one unavoidably sees the limits of the other. Some of these limits may, indeed, be defects of character and, consequently, admit of correction. Others, on the contrary, are manifestations of an existential contingency for which in principle no remedy is possible. Now if one has made the other his end in the sense being discussed, it becomes impossible for him to accept any limitations, particularly those touching upon his expectations in regard the definitive satisfaction of his needs as a subject. This situation must inevitably result in a disillusionment that initiates the move to look elsewhere. Such a move obviously must force a reclaiming of freedom--the freedom to look. And like the will to total freedom, it initiates the endless and restless journey into the unreal, the world that cannot be.

E.

I now wish to conclude these reflections on alienation by briefly explicating their connection with the substance of Essay 7. The existence of the human being is in itself unnecessary and on its own resource it can never be otherwise. Nevertheless, the form of its self-presence as at least inchoatively the form of personality is, due to its connaturality to existence, absolute. There is no other form from which or in relation to which it has significance, importance, or the authority to be actual. And mind's act of self-presence involves its awareness of both the frailty of itself as act and the absolute character of the form of this act. Furthermore, the mind's will to be is, as I have tried to show, a will to be perfectly actual as an act of existence to the extent of possibility determined by its form. Now, rightly conceived, this is an interest in the absolute for the purpose of maximal actualization through the participation of similitude. In other words, it is an interest, not in becoming an existential absolute which for it is impossible, but in the participation in such an absolute. Mind, of course, is encouraged in this direction by its own form of self-presence which both lays out the rule by which such participation is possible and certifies the authenticity of the rule through its evident sanctity. And being itself also indicates to intellect the existence of "He who is" in personal relation with whom in some way, not yet clarified, the mind's interest can be satisfied through identification and indwelling under the form of personality.

These three attitudes, however, obstruct this possibility although not all in the same way. Each involves a mistaken judgment about the absolute. The failure to take practical considerations into account in the decision to establish a relationship is, in effect, an attempt to make human love omnipotent and, by implication, an absolute. The will to total freedom quite obviously makes freedom the greatest value and, again by implication, attempts to make the subject of freedom an absolute. The expectation that the other can be one's finality requires of the other that he at least fulfill the role of an absolute. All three, therefore, necessarily misdirect what might be called the mind's life energies away from the real absolute and cause them to be spent on a fiction. In all three cases the inevitable result is the same, i.e., a frustration of the will to be that sooner or later must become a hatred of being.

In spite of this similarity, however, there are differences among the ways these attitudes obstruct the will to be that are of profound importance. The first attitude is childish. It is due to a perception about love that has been improperly conceptualized. As I have tried to show, the mind is vitally attracted to love because it correctly believes that in this situation it is to find the fullest satisfaction of its will to be. The form of personality which is actualized in love is both the form of the subject's access to the real absolute and the form of its maximal actualization. It is understandable, therefore, that the inexperienced person might make a mistake about just what love can and cannot do. Of the three attitudes, this is the most innocent in its intention and the most correctable in its consequences.

The third attitude is stupid. It expects of another who is plainly and beyond doubt in the same situation as oneself that which is clearly beyond one's own resource to provide for anyone. It is the calculated substitution of a fiction for the serious business of finding and relating to the real absolute. What is most contemptable about this attitude both in life and in literature is its attempt to canonize the stupidity and triviality of its judgment by connecting it with the very real importance of the human catastrophy that is its consequence. It is quite understandable that the lazy and silly selfishness of this attitude leads to the will to total freedom.

The second attitude is vicious. So long as it prevails, it makes the mind absolutely hostile to good and truth. As I have tried to indicate, this mind is completely evil in its intention and in its consequence. It not only misdirects its vital efforts toward a fiction, it makes itself in the process absolutely incompatible with that absolute whose essence is to exist and, therefore, who is both good and truth subsistent.

ESSAY 9

THE FINAL QUESTION

A.

We turn now to a completion of those considerations that occupied our attention in Essay 7. The relation of self-presence is the form of the act of existence as master of itself and, therefore, as being in its most authentic sense. It is the form of this act as being itself precisely through itself as having itself. This is the form of existence as intellectual and, therefore, as open to all being. In short, it is the form of the act of existence as encompassing.

The self-consciousness of mind is the actuality of its being to itself. This being to itself is, indeed, self-presence and indwelling, but as alone. This being to itself is meant to be sustained in the actuality of mind's being to another being to itself by which it realizes the form of personality and constitutes itself a name, as a who. In and by this act, it achieves the actuality of being an attitude to a person. It is this actuality that is designated by a personal name distinct from and in no way predicable of essence. Its name announces the actuality it has in the reality of its relation to another being to itself.

This form of existence as to itself is a part of the form of personality, i.e., the form of the order of being as a relation. This is the form of being as personal. That is to say, being personal is the act of which this is the form. The form of personality is the form of the act of existence as intellectual; it is the form of intellectual existence as self-conscious attitude toward another. This form gives being the greatest amplitude of actuality of which it is capable. The perfection of the actuality of the self-relation precisely as relation requires an other for the fulfillment of the form of personality.

Now the question must be asked, what is it about the form of self-presence that makes it practically (if not theoretically) clear to every mind that in the personal order of reality it is only a fragment of a larger unity, and that it is in this larger unity alone that it can achieve the actuality designated by a proper or personal name. Why does the form of self-presence need to be completed in the form of a relation with a real altereity? What is the metaphysical source of this necessity? Why is the subject by itself formally incomplete so that it cannot achieve the perfect actuality of its self-presence, i.e., a name, except in a relation to a real altereity as being to it. What is it about the self-relation of existence as intellectual that requires a real relation to an altereity as its perfect likeness. There must be something about the act of existing as such that finds the form of personality most congenial and connatural to its perfection and manifests itself in intellectual being's encompassing as the law of its complete reality.

These questions can be answered as follows. The self-relation is not a relation to itself precisely as relation. This would be impossible since no relation can refer to itself as such. So, from the metaphysical point of view, full perfection of existence precisely as being in relation requires that it be to a perfect likeness of itself, i.e., to another being to itself as standing in relation to the whole of me including and primarily that which is most me, my self-relation. In other words, I can achieve the complete unity of my being through a total encompassing which would include the reality of my self-relation if I indirectly, as it were, relate to that whole through the altereity of a likeness that is itself in relation to me as encompassing. It is, however, only in and according to the form of personality or identification that the real interrelation of several relations, sustained by the original term of <u>self</u> which, as such, is not a relation, allows for this maximal unity of being. This ultimate unity is expressed by the personal names.

      To put this another way. The act of existing in the being to itself is the actuality of the relation of the intellectual being to itself as both substance and act, but not as self-relation. The perfection of this actuality, therefore, precisely as that of the encompassing unity of self-presence cannot be realized merely in the solitary situation because a being cannot be in an encompassing relation to its relation of self-presence through that relation itself. Mind is present to itself, but not present <u>to</u> this presence; it is only present <u>in</u> this presence. The perfect unity of being as intellectual is its total encompassing self-presence which is possible only through the form of personality. Only in the situation of the mutual interpresence of several relations of self-presence is the entire reality of the intellectual being encompassed and thereby totally unified.

      From the very nature of the intellectual being's mode of unity as self-relation and from the impossibility of a relation relating to itself directly, the full and perfect actuality of the unity of such a being requires a relation of its self-presence to another self-presence according to the form of identification. It is only in this form of personality that the intellectual being's unity is perfectly actual and complete. This form allows for the most perfect unity of being because it constitutes the formal possibility of identification. It is the ultimate or absolute "essence," so to speak, of unity as such, and for this reason is connatural to the act of existing as such. The full realization of the perfection of this act is possible only through this form.

      This is the situation in which the intellectual being has a name that designates this perfect connatural unity of the act of presence. The name expresses the subject's perfect identity or unity. The actualization of this form gives the act by which it is actualized a participation in the existential necessity which belongs to the form absolutely in virtue of the primacy of its connaturality to existence as such. The perfection of the actuality of the form manifests itself uniquely not merely as goodness but precisely as sanctity. The perfection and, therefore, goodness of the perfection of existence in this form is absolute. Personality is the form of the most perfect unity possible for existence and, as such, maximizes the actuality of its perfection and goodness.

At the bottom of all this is the metaphysical claim that the form of personality is that form which in virtue of itself gives being the most perfect unity possible and is, therefore, the exemplar of all other forms of unity. As such, it enjoys a primacy of connaturality to existence as most perfectly actualizing its perfection and goodness. In other words, the complex nondiagrammatic relational situation of interpersonal identification of being as intellectual is the relational possibility of absolute and complete unity. Only the complex form of personality can provide existence with that self-encompassing unity that is both absolute and total. It is only in and through this form that existence as most perfectly itself, i.e., as intellectual, is fully real. Indeed, the being of the being to or the actuality of the attitude as such, which is this form is the perfect formal similitude of the act of existing as such and at its best. In other words, the actuality of this unity is precisely the maximized actuality of the existence of the being or beings of which it is the unity. The act of existing whose form does not limit its perfection by being really distinct from it is an act of being personal. This act is the form of personality as subsisting. The complete perfection of the unity of the actuality of self-presence therefore necessarily involves a real altereity of attitudes toward precisely as attitude.

Throughout this consideration I have been careful not to say that the altereity required by this form, although real, is necessarily existential. The form as such calls merely for an altereity that is relationally real. By this I mean that the relations are really different in virtue of some opposition and not simply in virtue of being in existentially different subjects. For example, the two relations that structure the situation of origin are really different precisely as relations, i.e., due to relational opposition, and not merely becuase of some existential difference of subjects. In other words, they are really different precisely as relations.

This point is of considerable importance. The finite subject cannot discover in its own consciousness that real altereity and confrontation of relations in which a real other claims all of this to be his as well as yours, or that it is all ours. As a practical consequence, this subject must look for and to an existentially different subject in order to actualize the form of personality. Now what I want to say is that one must not conclude from this necessity that the form of personality requires such an existential altereity. It does not. All that it demands precisely as form is the real opposition and distinction of relations.

That intellectual act by which and in which I am self-present is not identical with the substantial act of the existence of any being. I cannot properly say that I am my intellectual act. The ultimate reason for this, of course, is the real difference between my substantial act of existing and my essence. I cannot say that my essence is to exist. Therefore, I cannot say that any of my essential actions are my existence. Nevertheless, the form of this self-presence, as an inchoative participation in the unique and ultimate unity of the form of personality, gives the actuality of this presence a kind of substantiality in the sense that it makes it most me. It gives it the beginning of that total self-encompassing unity that is connatural to existence in its perfection.

My actuality (subsistent existence, actions, and relations) as intellectual involves a presence of itself to itself. That is to say, such actuality involves intellectual consciousness of both the existence and this consciousness itself. It involves a relation of the subject of intellectual consciousness to the full domain of the being of which it is the subject. The originating term of this relation is transcendental apperception. This is the Ego. It is the absolute unity of mind and, as such, speaks both itself and everything else of which mind is conscious. It is that self-conscious unity which claims for its own all that is me and all that is in me.

Now the "Ego" that is spoken by this transcendental apperception is the representation of the speaker in its consciousness of both the subsistent actuality and the unity of the being of which it is the subject. This spoken "Ego," however, cannot itself stand in the same kind of relation of unifying presence to the whole of consciousness because it cannot itself, as representation, be existentially identical with the original speaking apperception. In other words, in the finite mind there is no other real subject of consciousness by which all of consciousness could look back to the original apperception. In short, by itself, the subject of the finite mind is radically alone.

The reason for this solitude is that in the finite mind, although (as I have said above) the relation of the subject's presence to the whole domain of its reality (excepting, of course, this relation itself) is given a quasi-substantiality due to its being an originative element in the form of personality, the act of intellectual consciousness is not identical with, but rather really distinct from, the subject's substantial act of existing. Consequently, it is absolutely impossible for the mind's representation of its subjectivity ever to be or become a real and distinct other subject in its consciousness. In other words, no representation by transcendental apperception of itself in a finite mind can ever be the real subject of a real relation of presence to mind and everything in it (including and especially the relation of the original apperception).

It is of the essence of the rational being that it be present to itself as transcendental apperception and that this Ego be the subject of all its actions, states, and relations. But precisely because this finite essence is distinct from the substantial act of existing, no likeness or representation that mind can express of its own subjectivity can itself be a subject of that mind because it is not and cannot be a perfect likeness of the subject it represents. Regardless of what it represents, it is a thought and, as such, must be existentially distinct from that which thinks it. Therefore, it must be existentially distinct from the existence of the subjectivity of mind. Existentially it belongs to the plurality of mind and not to its apperceptive unity. Precisely because it must be existentially distinct from the actuality of this apperceptive subject, it is impossible for it to be a real subject of that mind. If, by hypothesis, this thought were to be a real subject, it would follow from its existential distinction from the actuality of the original apperceptive subject that it would have to also constitute another mind. In brief, because my essence and my substantial act of existing are not one and the same, there is also a corresponding difference between this act and the intellectual activity through which I am present to myself. This difference, then, carries with it the further limiting consequence that no other identity can be found in this act than the original apperception.

From this it follows that it is absolutely impossible for the finite mind, precisely because it is finite, that is to say, precisely because of the reality of the distinction between its essence and its existence, to possess within itself the necessary condition for the actualization of the form of personality, i.e., real altereity of subjects. And from this it of course follows further that the only possible way the finite mind can achieve the unity and actuality of which this form is the connatural condition is to turn to another existentially distinct subject for an interpersonal relationship. In the light of these considerations I hope it is clear that existential diversity of subjects is not a requirement of the form of personality but rather derives exclusively from the ontological condition of the finite mind.

B.

Now I think we are in a better position to directly address in its final form the questions introduced in Essay 7. If there is a being whose essence is to exist, who might he be and, from a metaphysical point of view, what would be the possibility and consequence of a personal relation with such a being? The first part of this question involves, of course, the difficult issue of knowing something in a definite way about such a being and, in the present context, knowing how such a being could be personal. Finite intelligence, even at its best, is limited in its manner of knowing by the manner of its existing. Precisely because its act of knowing, which is its actuality as mind, is distinct from the substantial existence of the being in which it occurs, it cannot grasp in any direct, univocal, and comprehensive thought the perfections or, more precisely, the perfection of the intellectuality of a being in which there is no such distinction.

To put this another way, that being in which the real distinction between its essence and its substantial existence restricts its conceptual competence to objects whose essences limit the perfection of their existence will naturally be capable of only some kind of analogical knowledge of the perfection of a being whose existence is its essence. Consequently, to ask how such a being can be personal which, from our point of view, is the highest possible unity and perfection is to set up the delicate task of saying neither more than one can possibly know nor denying anything that one can indeed know about a being whose mode of existence absolutely transcends our own.

That such a being must be in some sense intellectual is clear from the fact that, as the subsistent act of existing, it contains all possible perfection although in a transcendent manner. Indeed, it is for this reason not only intellectual but subsistently intellectual. Its intellectual act is its existence. But what this means positively as we move from our intellect which we know connaturally to an unlimited intellect is not immediately clear. Nevertheless, if intellect as we know it in ourselves reveals something about intellectuality in itself as a mode of being, and if self-presence by way of self-knowledge and self-love are essential to this intellectuality as such, then it would seem to be the case that "He who is" is present to himself. From this it would follow that the form of personality which is the necessary form of the perfect unity of self-presence is fully actualized in this being and, indeed, is identical with his act of existing.

Now if just this much can be admitted, we can take the matter one step further and say that the necessary condition for the actualization of this form must also be found in "He who is," i.e., the real distinction of multiple identity. As I have shown, this requirement of the form of personality does not of itself necessarily imply any sort existential difference between the relationally distinct identities and, therefore, the idea of real multiple identity is not incompatible with the absolute existential simplicity of a being whose essence is to exist.

These claims, although analogical, are of supreme importance to the ultimate interests of metaphysics. Existence as act *per se* and as perfection is metaphysically clearer to us viewed through the form of personality than it is viewed through the form of essence. From the viewpoint of essence, being is seen as a what. It may, indeed, be taken as an intellectual thing that is, in virtue of its intellectuality, capable of being personal. Nevertheless, from this perspective the focus is on the intellectuality of its various operations rather than on the personality of certain relations that are involved in or follow upon these operations. In other words, in this perspective the focus is on the what aspect of the being and the operations proper to that aspect.

Viewed, however, through the form of personality, i.e., through the form of who rather than what, through indeed the form of the most perfect unity and goodness, the focus is on those personal relations which are involved in the various intellectual operations by which the being is present to itself. The focus, in other words, is on existence as the actuality of attitude toward rather than on the actuality of the action itself. From this perspective the act of existence of the absolute being is seen as the act of being personal according to the form of personality. In other words, the perspective of the absolute being as the subsistent actuality of immanent relations according to the form of personality gives greater clarity to its existence through the unity and holiness of that form. The consideration of "He who is" from the perspective of the primacy of who over what yields greater metaphysical insight into existence as perfection than does essence precisely because it looks primarily on the act of existing as subsistent attitude rather than on this act as operation. In this perspective, the special character of the connatural unity of being as intellectual (i.e., as self-present) can be seen more clearly.

As a matter of fact, essence itself as form becomes clearer in this connection when viewed as the form of the existential necessity of the form of personality. In this instance, the essence perfectly expresses the necessity of existence and thereby the necessity of the primary form of existence. Just as the form of personality is the proper connatural form of the absolute perfection of the subsistent act of existing, that is to say, is this act as absolutely perfect, so the essence "to exist" is seen to express the necessity of the actuality of this form. It must be actual. That is why "He who is" is <u>essentially</u> holy. So, it belongs to that being whose essence is to exist to be self-sufficiently personal, i.e., to be in and through itself the full actualization of the complete form of personality.

C.

Now there must be some existentially grounded capacity for the recognition of the authenticity of the names if and when they are given over and above the characteristic of the event mentioned at the end of Essay 7. These identities are by their essence that self-subsisting act of existence that is the being whose essence is to exist. They are the persons who uniquely and by absolute necessity not only are the ones who are present to each other in the self-presence that is this act, the actuality of their interpersonal realtions is this existence. They are indeed those indentities who, in virtue of the perfection of the form of their relationship as actualized in one absolutely simple act of existing (or existing to), must be. They necessarily exist, from our point of view, because of who they are. They are subsistent "to be persons" (or personal), and this is why they are subsistent "to be."

It is necessary, therefore, that finite intellectual beings whose mode of existence is a participation in the unity of the form of existence--encompassing self-presence and who, as intellectual, are open to all being, would have as their ultimate essential metaphysical interest to find out who "He who is" may be precisely as present to himself in order to be able to know him personally and thereby achieve a definitive self-actualization. It is also necessary that, due to their participation in existence through the similitude of a self-encompassing radical personality, they must have a connatural disposition for recognizing these names when given as being who the existence is in which they participate.

We participate by similitude in that existence which, as such, is the subsistent actualization of that form of personality which is radically and inchoatively present in our own essence as intellectual and which we, therefore, are meant to actualize in a limited way as the form of the ultimate unity of our being. My intellectual presence to my existence and its essence is the basis, therefore, of my capacity to recognize the authenticity of the identities of that reality of which I am a finite likeness. In other words, my essential interest in being a person involves an equally essential interest in the identities of those persons whose reality constitutes the ontological ground of the form of personality just, indeed, as their act of existing, from the point of view of essence, constitutes the ontological ground of being as existence. And so, the finite intellectual being's ultimate metaphysical concern is to discover and relate to these identities in order to definitively maximize the unity of its being and, thereby, definitively stabilize and secure its existence. This same finite being's ultimate cognitive capacity, rooted in the intellectuality of its existence, is its connatural sense for recognizing the authenticity of the names of the identities whose reality is precisely that subsistent act of existing (of being personal) in which it participates by similitude.

To know this being merely by the name "He who is" is not and cannot be sufficient for a perfect personal relationship. This name indicates to us only the uniqueness of his existence in regard to its ontological status. It does not indicate to us the absolute uniqueness of the unity of that existence in virtue of the relating of its self-presence or its self-encompassing. In other words, as a name, it announces no identity as grounded in existence as the act of being personal or as the actuality of the form of personality. Consequently, it is impossible for us, given the limitation of the human mind, to have a perfect relation of identification with this being on the basis of this name alone. For such a relation, I must know who he is in his self-presence in order to relate to him in my self-presence. As I have said, however, theoretical mind has absolutely no access to these proper names. Only if they are personally given can one know their real content. Nevertheless, it can be shown that they must indeed be given, at least if wanted, and that, as a consequence, the perfect satisfaction of the mind's will to be is a possibility grounded in the ultimate structure of being.

The existential character of the absolutely uncompromising respect for dignity is, as we have seen in Essay 7, holiness. That being whose essence is to exist is, therefore, absolutely holy. In fact, its existence as the actuality of that interrelation of its identities which constitutes the unity of its self-encompassing is an act of respect. In other words, this being is not only holy, it is "to be holy."

As we have already seen, however, the essential ontological status of the rational being is that of dignity. This dignity, again as we have seen, is the absolute worth and authority of existence as the radical perfection precisely as maximized in and expressed through its most connatural form, i.e., the form of encompassing self-presence. This is, of course, the source, thrust, and form of the mind's will to be. This will is not just another, albeit more complex, force in nature. This will, precisely because of the form of consciousness in which it occurs, is existence asserting its radical perfection, asserting that it is in itself absolutely good, and asserting that this goodness is the source of an unqualified or categorical authority to be, to be maximally itself, to be maximally perfect, to be therefore maximally actual. The actuality of a being is, however, a reciprocal of its unity. And for the encompassing self-present being, the form of its most perfect unity is that of personality. This form, however, for reasons we have already considered, requires real altereity of identity. For the finite subject, this means its ultimate perfection and actuality depends on a personal relation with an identity existentially different from its own.

That ultimate definitive maximization of the actuality of the subject which is achieved through the form of its encompassing unity is possible only in a relationship with identities whose act of existence is the original subsistent actuality of that form. To complete one's encompassing unity through a relationship with persons whose essence is to exist and whose existence is the original subsistent actualization of the form of personality would give that unity an existential stability it cannot achieve with another finite subject. Furthermore, this unity itself, precisely as unity, would be more perfect because it would be a function of an actualization of the form of personality with persons who are that original subsistent act of existence of which I am a limited participating likeness. In other words, identification based on this transcendent similitude must produce in the finite subject's self-encompassing unity a transcendent authenticity that is absolutely impossible in any other relationship.

The essential status of the intellectual being is dignity. This dignity, which is this kind of being's absolute worth and authority to exist, is resident in and expressed by encompassing self-presence as both the form and the interest of its will to be. In fact, this will to be is the actualization of dignity as self-consciousness. This will contains, therefore, the finite mind's transcendent essential affinity to the being whose essence is to exist. As we have just seen, however, it is impossible for this will to be perfectly and definitively fulfilled without access to the personal identities of "He who is." As we have also seen, "He who is" is essentially holy. His act of existence is respect for dignity. The holiness, therefore, of this being necessarily involves respect for the finite intellectual subject's will to be. The absolute holiness of that being whose essence is to exist cannot obstruct the finite intellectual being's authority to be. Its holiness compels the giving of these names on the ground of affinity, if they are wanted. It is absolutely impossible for "He who is" to refuse to be fully personal to any intellectual being that would want such a relationship.

A relation of the kind I have been discussing would have to be a participation on the part of the finite subject in the interpersonal relationship of these identities. These identities constitute a We that is the explicitation of the perfection of the unity of their mutual self-encompassing. Now for the finite subject to participate in this unity, i.e., to become included in the We, it must relate in a way fundamentally similar to the way they relate to each other. This basic way is, of course, that of absolute respect. This attitude is the necessary ground of a communality in the order of identity that can be formalized into the unity of We.

The identities of the being whose essence is to exist constitute the personal unity of its act of respect for its own infinite dignity. Because they do not *have* their existence as we do but rather *are* that existence personally, they do not have dignity as we do but rather each *is* that dignity in the very uniqueness of who it *is*. In this sense, each of these persons, precisely as who it is, is subsistent goodness. Also, because these identities do not *have* respect for this good as personified in each other but rather each *is* that respect, they are in their names subsistently holy. The actuality, therefore, of the form of personality in this being is the act of respect for its infinite dignity, and this act is indeed its entire existence. This is why it is the case that for these identities to be who they are is to be holy.

D.

Now, as I have said, if the finite subject is to be included in this We, it must relate to its constitutive identities in the same way they relate to each other, i.e., with absolute respect for the dignity that each has in virtue of who it is. It must respect each identity or name as being personally the infinite dignity of that substantial act of existence that is its own complete and perfect encompassing. That is to say, the finite subject must relate through that act of specific name-oriented respect by which it is personal to each of these identities and through which it becomes holy. This attitude and its consequent sanctification of the mind that has it is the necessary common ontological ground for the communality expressed by We. It is this similitude that allows for a relation of identification between these identities and the finite subject in which the latter participates in the actuality of the form of personality of the being whose essence is to exist.

It is in this situation that the finite subject completes its encompassing unity and thereby is a name. This name announces the complete unity of the encompassing self-presence precisely as unique. But in this case, the name is transcendent because the relation upon which it is based is one toward persons whose essence is to exist. Indeed, the name is transcendent because it is a participation in a relationship the essence of whose actuality is to exist. From the point of view of metaphysics, this is the most critical moment for the finite mind's will to be because it is in precisely this moment that it has real access to the real existential absolute. It is in this moment that the mind is to find, at least inchoatively, the full definitive satisfaction of all those interests we normally call metaphysical.

It is also in this situation that the finite subject achieves the fullest authenticity of its substantial actuality. Its categorical determination to respect absolutely the dignity of the identities who are their existence is the ultimate verification (in the literal sense of that word) of its own existence as intellectual. It is existence precisely as absolutely true to itself. As a direct consequence, it participates fully in the existential authority to be, not just in virtue of its essence but now precisely in virtue of its identity. As who it is, and not just as what it is, it ought to be.

There is, of course, an immediate connection between the completeness of unity expressed by the personal name of the subject and the authenticity or sanctity of its substantial existence. First, both the unity and the authenticity are functions of the form of personality and are due to that form's affinity or proximity to the act of existence as perfection. Second, the conjunction of the two in a finite subject constitutes its ontological integrity. In this situation, it is wholly what being is about at its best. That is to say, it is real.

It would seem to be the case, however, that death and its unavoidability totally negate this integrity. Of what use is unity and authenticity to a being that will certainly die? Death in general is simply the end of a living organism's ability to hold itself together and to act. Its unity, that which makes it what it is, has lost its grip. Death, precisely as human, is the end of the control of the subject's essential form over the mode of its being. This form prescribes certain plays that must be acted out by each individual. The scripts for these plays do not seem to have changed significantly in over half a million years. From time to time they are acted out with an unusual insight that is of permanent importance to the human family, but for the most part, the level of performance remains predictably much the same. In any case, the scripts themselves remain exactly the same.

These scripts possess, however, only a very limited content with respect to the scope and interest of mind. There is, after all, only so much one can find to hold mind's attention in conception, birth, puberty, sex, family, aging, illness, and death, not to mention politics, business, entertainment, crime, natural disasters, and war, etc. The intellect easily becomes bored with both the original script and its repetition. Nobody in his right mind would want to avoid death if that involved an indefinite continuation of this. The human being transcends this program and, because he transcends it, gives it whatever limited importance it may possess. We naturally and rightly expect something better to come out of it and to replace it. Hence the ontology of human death.

The essential form of the human being which prescribes this program and through this prescription determines the mode or style of our existing betrays its fundamental inadequacy in regard to the ultimate interests of mind as intellectual. It cannot of itself provide the individual with the unity and authenticity that it requires for the perfection of its actuality as a self-presence. It is the principle of a routine that is incapable of responding to intellect's self-conscious openness to being. It is, in short, by its own very limitation, both at a distance from existence as perfection and incommensurate with the interests of intellect. It does not and cannot fit existence as intellectual.

The form of personality, on the other hand, precisely because of its affinity to existence as perfection, is commensurate with these interests of intellect. Furthermore, the integrity achieved by the finite subject through the form of personality is evidence for mind that the actualization of the primacy of this form over human essence inchoatively removes the latter's control over the mode of one's existing and guarantees the ultimate definitive transcendent integrity of the finite being. In other words, this is the gradual emergence in the essence dominated program of scenes of the transcendent primacy of the form of personality in regard to both the integrity and the mode of the finite being. In this perspective, death is seen ontologically as the finite subject's ultimate liberation from the inadequacy of the essential mode of existence and the definitive accomplishment of the personal mode. Death may be feared both in regard to its circumstances and in regard to the separation it entails. But in itself, it possesses that special beauty that belongs only to the very first moment of my great completion.

The completed and perfect actualization of the form of personality includes and must include the immediate intellectual vision of the existence and essence of that being whose essence is to exist. First, I must see the existence and essence of the other in order for the unity of my encompassing self-presence to be perfect, i.e., for the completion of the unity of my self-presence through my relation to the other. No perfect self-presence is possible through an incomplete relation to the other.

Second, the relation itself to "He who is" requires that I see him as he is in order for there to exist in me that similitude to himself required by this kind of relation. Since he is precisely his act of seeing his existence, I cannot be adequately similar to him for the completeness of the form of personality if, unlike him, I do not see his existence and essence. In such a defective situation, the unity of We must of necessity be incomplete. Third, my personal knowledge of the identities of the being whose essence is to exist is imperfect if I do not see that existence and its identity with its essence which each of their identities is personally. I cannot have that knowledge of them by name required for the complete participation in their form of personality if I do not see the existence that is the act of this form.

Fourth, this vision is the only way intellectual consciousness, given its openness to being, can become completely actual and thereby capable of a perfect relation of encompassing self-presence. "He who is" is the only reality that in virtue of both its essence and its form of personality allows its act of existence the scope of absolute perfection and intelligibility. No other reality, therefore, is able to satisfy mind's metaphysical interest in its own being by giving it the actuality required for a definitive and perfect presence to itself.

The possibility of this seeing is, of course, grounded in the connatural affinity of the intellect for this being as a consequence of the ontological assimilation of the finite subject to it because of the unity and sanctity or authenticity it achieves in the form of personality. Through the act of its personal knowing of these identities and both because this knowing involves an assimilation of the knower to the known and because these identities are their existence, the finite subject moves to vision. This move, however, cannot be completed until the definitive primacy of the form of personality in regard to mode has been established. Until that moment occurs, the intellect's mode of knowing, although inchoatively connatural to that of the form of personality through its actively being personal, is still "bound" to that of the form of the human essence. Only death gives it freedom from the limits of this mode. This is the transcendent freedom that can be achieved only by the investment of the mind's natural freedom in the self-limitation of respect. This is the freedom to see.

ESSAY 10

STATES OF MIND AND KNOWING

There are several topics yet outstanding which taken together might be called "epistemological," at least in some very broad understanding of that term. I now wish to offer the reader my thoughts on these subjects, but only insofar as those thoughts bear directly on the central interest of these Essays as a whole. Hopefully without serious prejudice to the other important philosophical aspects of the interpersonal relation, I have concentrated on the properly metaphysical. With this in mind, the following reflections are presented not primarily as epistemology but rather for the purpose of rounding out this treatment and thereby bringing it to a suitable conclusion.

A. Sympathy

The organic unity of self-present consciousness is such that there exists a sympathy among its various powers which enables a dominant activity in one to stimulate corresponding reactions in the others. That is to say, the affinity among the domains of thought, attitude, feeling, and mood makes it possible for activity in one to directly stimulate corresponding activity in the others. This sympathetic correspondence whereby consciousness maintains its unity among the plurality of its modes may be viewed as a translating of dominant events in the language of one power into the proper languages of all the others. Peace is the sense of either the success or the possibility of success of this integrative activity. It is the sense of being as unified or focused act. Restlessness is the sense of the failure of the integrative activity and is, therefore, the sense of self as nonbeing relative to its existence as unity.

B. Mystique

Because of this sympathetic harmony, events in one domain can have power over the whole field of consciousness. There can be established through sympathetic unity a prevailing mentality or cast of mind the logic of which constitutes a real force in all the domains toward a particular set of possibilities as translations. This kind of harmonic resonance of consciousness with some dominant event I call its mystique. This is unity as a force in consciousness. It is a constellation of dispositions generated and controlled by some powerful event in consciousness through the apperceptive unity of mind. This is unity as power, as a net of forces. The distinctive profile of any mystique is personality.

Ego is the self-consciousness of self-presence. As a mind state, its unity (which it is) is the consciousness of the success of its activity of unification (which it is). Ego is the conscious unity of the translating activity across the whole field of consciousness. As formal consciousness, it is the sense of unity imposing itself on mobile consciousness the self-awareness of which activity as successful is its life. To fail is to die, to cease to be what it is, a unity. Ego-unity in this fundamentally most important sense is the source of mind's interest in the total harmony of its prevailing mystique.

Ego, however, is not merely unity through coherence of meanings. It is also unity through power to control its events. Mind not only knows itself; it also rules itself. It unifies itself through self-possession. It has, therefore, a specific interest in its unity as power. Failure in this regard is the non-being of Ego as self-possessor. Mystique is, therefore, important to Ego both in regard to its fit with other events in consciousness establishing sense that is coherent and in regard to strength or power to hold mind together.

The sympathy of consciousness is a dynamic for the unity of harmony throughout the total range of consciousness such that the logic of the prevailing mystique fits the logic of events in the various domains. When this situation is the case, the unity of identity in Ego is secure and there is a sense of peace throughout consciousness. If, however, there is either a tension between the prevailing mystique and the logic of some strong event elsewhere in consciousness, or (and this is by far the more serious situation) if two contrary mystiques begin to exist in the same consciousness, the unitary consciousness of the Ego is threatened and there results unrest and turbulence.

The former situation is usually characterized by much specious rationalizing or efforts to suppress the event out of attention. The latter, however, represents the ultimate danger to mind. The vacillation of the Ego between two powerful mystiques that cannot be synthesized eventuates in a fundamental loss of apperceptive control. In such a case, a powerful event in any domain of consciousness can reinstate the contrary mystique and the Ego becomes trapped or "possessed." Mystique which should be the Ego's net of control over all of consciousness and thereby correlatively the stability of its identity, becomes the destruction of that identity. The Ego is the optic or focal point of the unity of the mystique. The radical shift from one mystique to a rival one involves a radical shift in optics within consciousness. Ultimately, it represents the generation of conflicting identities within the same conscious being. The unity is destroyed. The unitary optic is lost.

C. Empathy

Just as the identity of Ego-consciousness is a function of the coherence of its mystique, so the identity of We-consciousness is a function of the compatibility of the mystiques of the several subjects involved. In those cases where there exists a high degree of similarity between the dominant mystiques an intimate mutual relationship becomes possible and, indeed, name-constitution in the most fundamental ontological sense actually occurs. I call this affinity of mystiques empathy. On the other hand, where there are radically opposed mystiques intimate unification of identities in the order of name is impossible. In this context only impersonal relationships are possible. Substantive communication is impossible because there is no common optic. This is why love without friendship usually ends in alienation.

D. Mystique and Truth Attitudes

Allowing that the rule making power of mind can as a matter of fact construct virtually any formula it wants, it seems that the ultimate real reason for chosing in any particular case one set of rules over another is interest or rather double interests. Mind choses certain rules over others because it wants to succeed at something it is interested in doing. It also choses rules with an eye to their fit with the rest of the rules it uses in other domains of interest. In both cases, the interest is inspired to a greater or less degree by mystique.

The choice of rules, tacit or explicit, governing communication, verification, values, and beliefs is controlled by these two interests. We select and build up truth attitudes, value attitudes, and language as a function of our interests. The relationship between mystique, interest, and rule choice is important because rules for the admissibility of data as confirmatory evidence relative to various kinds of theories whose selection was sympathetic in origin may in turn influence the formation of the rules for the admissibility of meaning or sense. That is to say, rules for verification will tend to put pressure on the choices of rules for recognition of discourse as significant so that certain kinds of discourse may be declared meaningless because they do not fit the interests determining the rules for verification.

From the perspective that generated the verification rules, they are uninteresting. Eventually this could project itself into a theory of human knowing that would leave no room for the kinds of cognitive claims we wish to make in these essays.

E. Mystical Knowing

The prevailing mystique functions as an influence for or against cognitive events and attitudes depending on their sympathetic and empathetic impact on its logic. Insights, beliefs, symbol activity, and personal knowing will be re-enforced or resisted by the prevailing mystique. So, mystique fundamentally affects the cognitive domain. Conversely, sufficiently powerful events in the cognitive domain can effect a radical change of mystique. The latter revolution in consciousness involves both a metamorphosis of personality and a corresponding shift in the apperceptive optic of the subject that may in some instances (e.g., when the cognitive event is in the personal order) be so radical as to generate a new name or who-consciousness.

I would reserve the word "mystical" to designate all and only those events in consciousness or those aspects of events in consciousness that result from sympathetic harmonization with an extraordinary event elsewhere in consciousness. In this sense of the word, mystical events need not be religious. They can also be scientific, aesthetic, or personal. By "mystical knowing" I would mean those events in which consciousness as cognitive is sympathetically heightened to the level of the intensity of the act achieved elsewhere in mind and achieves knowledge appropriate to the optic of the mystique of that act. Mystical knowing is religious only when the mystique of the originating event is religious.

F. Faith

Faith belongs to that mystique within whose optic cognitive events of the personal order become possible which are seen to be the perfect to-be and life of the subject. The generation of this mystique is the result of a total sympathetic harmonization with the affirmation that this attitude contains the possibility for the perfect unification of mind the consciousness of which is the existence of the Ego. It is seen to be and accepted as the true way to be because it is seen to perfectly fulfill mind's ontological interest in truth. To know is an aspect of the act of the existence of the Ego. In the case of faith, the affinity of all the domains of consciousness with the ontological interest of the subject moves the mind to accept as true that which in the act of its acceptance perfectly fulfills mind's interest in truth. In other words, the ground of mind's serious interest in any truth moves it to assume this attitude as the way for rational mind to be.

The generation of this mystique is also the result of the mind's total sympathetic harmonization with the sense of the holiness of the event in which a person offers himself to another in an invitation to love and also the holiness of the optic within which this person and invitation become visible. I perceive that this mystique offers, therefore, not only the possibility of perfect unity of consciousness the awareness of which is the I that I am, but also the possibility of a modality of absolute importance for that act as such. In other words, the ground of mind's interest in any necessity moves it to accept this attitude as the way for it to be.

The knowledge achieved in faith is, therefore, mystical because it is an act of judgment whose justification is the sympathetic affinity of the knowing capacity with mind's apperceptive sensitivity to something's ability to satisfy its absolute ontological interests in unity and necessity.

G. Knowledge of God's Existence

The thought by which one interpretively views scientific and aesthetic knowing as getting through the structures of reality and the splendor of existence to the signature of a personal, necessary, all present being of whom reality is to some degree a likeness authenticates itself to consciousness as its natural optic by satisfying its apperceptive need for at least the possibility of perfect organic unity within itself and with the world. This optic enables consciousness to generate a mystique in which it integrates its felt need and will to exist necessarily and significantly, its sense of its own dignity, its interest in coherent values, its need for a total faithful love, its moral impulse, its inclination to a belief in the radical intelligibility of existence, and its feelings and moods in regard to nature. Its characteristics are lightsomeness and inner peace. Mind consciously structuring itself with this optic becomes sense by making sense to itself. The manifest good sense of adopting this perspective is sufficient subjective reason for its being adopted. Sanity itself urges its adoption. This enlightened self-interest is not, however, a "proof" of God's existence.

Although the sense of apperceptive unity and sympathetic peace within consciousness and with nature are not themselves direct evidence of God's existence, they do become indirect evidence when, after the primary evidence has been achieved, the knowledge of God's existence becomes itself generative of an absolutely dominant mystique within whose optic the human mind itself is seen to be a limited likeness of that being. In retrospect, so to speak, mind's scientific and aesthetic activities can be seen to be really a seeing through to the sanctity, intelligence, beauty, and power of the being whose essence is to exist. Within the perspective of the evidence of God's existence, the mind's original self-interest is confirmed by the fact that it becomes totally clear to itself and makes in that clarity final sense to itself. Knowledge of God's existence is, therefore, mystical, although not merely so.

H. Knowing God

Knowing "He who is" as an event in the order of personal knowing is possible only within the optic of the personalist mystique. To know someone is not reducible to knowing what x is, or how x is, or even who x is in the sense that one would know the public name by which x is called in his various public relationships. These are all instances of knowing a fact yielding information about x, and although the information can be forgotten and then relearned, there is no need for a continuing involved cognizing activity for such claims to be true.

When, however, the name that is known is not the social convention designating the individual and his public relationships but rather the name that he is, then knowing who he is is knowing the person. It is the apperceptive act as constituted by mind's unifying involvement with another apperceptive act also unifyingly involved with it in conscious mutuality. It is apperception become name-consciousness.

Empathy, or similarity of mystiques between persons is required for that sharing of the common optic without which the success of mutual name revelation would not be possible. Further, not only must the mystiques be similar; they must be similar precisely in that both have the profile of **respect** and openness to the other as their dominant structuring attitude. It is the community of this optic that makes union of interrelated name consciousness in the apperceptive order possible. That is to say, the apperceptive unity as consciousness of one's self as who (name) as being to the other as related to me depends upon my viewing the other in this way.

There is a sense, of course, in which all personal knowing is conditioned in its possibility upon this attitude and is, therefore, mystical. More than other kinds of knowing, personal knowing requires the focus of the whole consciousness. It is an act requiring the whole of orchestrated mind. This is why personal knowing when fully successful produces not only peace as a sense of being as perfectly unified internally, but also ecstacy, i.e., the sense of being "out" of one's limitations, of being infinite. This is also why serious failure of one's personal relationships produces extreme unrest and a Dark Night of consciousness.

      The immediacy of awareness on the part of finite subjects necessary for name communication in knowing God requires, however, not merely the optic of the mystique of openness, but precisely God's own mystique. Only similarity of mystiques (or spirits) that are in themselves holy makes the required optic for immediacy of awareness possible. Knowing God, therefore, is in the primary sense mystical.